The Golden Gems Of Life

An Updated and Abridged Version

of the original book by

S. C. Ferguson and E. A. Allen

Edited by

Doug Kenney

Published by PhiloSophia Publishing

ISBN-13: 978-0-9823221-1-6; ISBN-10: 0-9823221-1-9

Cover design by Jon Kenney

This book is dedicated to my children, Sarah, Jonathan, Daniel, and Philip. May you always seek wisdom in all that you do and pass along this desire from generation to generation.

Proverbs 2:1-4; 6
My child, listen to what I say, and treasure my commands.
Tune your ears to wisdom, and concentrate on understanding.
Cry out for insight, and ask for understanding.
Search for them as you would for silver; seek them like hidden treasures.
For the LORD grants wisdom! From his mouth come knowledge and understanding.

2 Chronicles 1:7-12
That night God appeared to Solomon and said, "What do you want? Ask, and I will give it to you!"
Solomon replied to God, "You showed great and faithful love to David, my father, and now you have made me king in his place. O LORD God, please continue to keep your promise to David my father, for you have made me king over a people as numerous as the dust of the earth! Give me the wisdom and knowledge to lead them properly, for who could possibly govern this great people of yours?"
God said to Solomon, "Because your greatest desire is to help your people, and you did not ask for wealth, riches, fame, or even the death of your enemies or a long life, but rather you asked for wisdom and knowledge to properly govern my people—I will certainly give you the wisdom and knowledge you requested. But I will also give you wealth, riches, and fame such as no other king has had before you or will ever have in the future!"

Proverbs 19:20
Get all the advice and instruction you can, and be wise the rest of your life.   (NLT)

Proverbs 23:24-25
The father of godly children has cause for joy. What a pleasure it is to have wise children. So give your parents joy! May she who gave you birth be happy.   (NLT)

Proverbs 3:13-18
Happy is the person who finds wisdom, the one who gets understanding. Wisdom is worth more than silver; it brings more profit than gold. Wisdom is more precious than rubies; nothing you could want is equal to it. With her right hand wisdom offers you a long life, and with her left hand she gives you riches and honor. Wisdom will make your life pleasant and will bring you peace. As a tree produces fruit, wisdom gives life to those who use it, and everyone who uses it will be happy.   (NCV)

Proverbs 8:12; 17-21
"I am wisdom, and I have the ability to think. I also have knowledge and good sense. I love those who love me. Those who want me find me. Riches and honor are mine. So are wealth and lasting success. What I give is better than the finest gold. What I give is better than pure silver. I do what is right. I do what is fair. I give wealth to those who love me. I fill them with treasures." (ICB)

INTRODUCTION 7

PREFACE...9

THE GIFT OF LIFE.......................................11

THE AIM OF LIFE 15

FAMILY LIFE 19

HOME   21
ADVICE TO PARENTS   23
ADVICE TO CHILDREN   32
LOVE LIFE   35
COURTSHIP   37
MARRIED LIFE   40
ADVICE TO HUSBANDS   47
ADVICE TO WIVES   49
MANHOOD   50
WOMANHOOD   52

VIRTUES TO ACQUIRE....................................58

DIGNITY OF WORK   59
PERSEVERENCE   61
ENERGY   64
ENTERPRISE   67
PUNCTUALITY   69
CONCENTRATION   71
DECISION   73
THE ABILITY TO THINK   75
A TRAINED MIND   76
WISE CHOICE OF COMPANIONS   85
FRIENDSHIP   86
GOOD HABITS   89
PERSONAL INFLUENCE   90
A GOOD CHARACTER   93
TRUE GREATNESS   99
FRUGALITY   101
PATIENCE   104
SELF-CONTROL   106
COURAGE   108
COMPASSION   110
KINDNESS   112
BENEVOLENCE   114
VERACITY   115
CONTENTMENT   117
POLITENESS   119

SOCIABILITY................................ 121
AFFABILITY................................. 123
OUTER ADORNMENT............................ 124
MEMORY..................................... 126
HAPPINESS.................................. 127
OPPORTUNITY................................ 130

VICES TO AVOID..................................133

VANITY..................................... 135
SELFISHNESS................................ 136
STUBBORNNESS............................... 137
SLANDER.................................... 139
IRRITABILITY............................... 141
ENVY....................................... 142
JEALOUSY................................... 143
DECEPTION.................................. 144
INTERMEDDLING AND GOSSIP................... 145
ANGER...................................... 147
AMBITION................................... 149

TRIALS OF LIFE..................................151

TRIALS..................................... 153
REGRET..................................... 156
PROSPERITY................................. 159
TRIFLES.................................... 161
LEISURE.................................... 163
SICKNESS................................... 166
SORROW..................................... 167
POVERTY.................................... 169
FAILURE.................................... 171

SPIRITUAL LIFE..................................177

FAITH...................................... 179
WORSHIP.................................... 180
THE BIBLE.................................. 183
GOD IN NATURE.............................. 185
FUTURE LIFE................................ 185

THE EVENING OF LIFE 187

APPENDIX......................................191

THE DAFFODIL PRINCIPLE***.................. 191
THE SEED................................... 195

INTRODUCTION

Have you ever heard someone say, "If I had my life to live over, I wouldn't change a thing?" I've always contended that those individuals are few and far between. We are human, which means we are prone to err—to make wrong or unwise decisions. You and I are fortunate to lay our head on the pillow at the end of even one day with no regrets.

Every now and then after reading a book, I will say to myself, "I sure wish I had read this book when I was younger." Perhaps if I had known and applied what I learned in the book, I would have done things differently and have fewer regrets.

Several years ago I read "The Golden Gems of Life." The beautiful language of the book and its timeless message captivated me. Although it was written in the late 1800s, the advice set forth in the book seemed just as applicable for my generation as it was for their generation and will be for future generations. It is a book full of wise counsel about life and how to live it to the fullest. In fact, when you read the preface to this book, you will see that the original authors desired that the people of our country would recognize the value of life, follow wise counsel, and live happy, productive, and successful lives.

The original book has over 600 pages. At the time I decided to republish the book, it was out of print, but my children found one of the original books at a used bookstore and gave it to me as a gift. I decided to publish an abridged version by eliminating repetition, reorganizing and combining some sections, and updating some of the words and phrases. I have done my best to capture the essence and intent of the message that the original authors wished to convey.

The wisdom you acquire as you live your life needs to be passed down to the next generation. As you read this book, I encourage you to highlight passages and write notes containing your own thoughts. You never know who may pick up this book in the future and read it—benefiting not only from the words of the authors, but also the words *you* write on these pages.

For you to benefit the most from this book, its words *and* the thoughts that come to your mind as you read should be meditated upon and then applied to your own life. To learn more about how to do this, read the section on A Trained Mind (pg. 76; specifically pgs. 83-84).

The best legacy you can leave those who follow you is a life well-lived—an example they can follow. If you are still young, you have the opportunity to begin well *and* finish well. However, if you already have regrets from the life you have lived thus far, it is never too late to change your course and finish well. Begin now to apply the "gems" inside this book, and from this day forward live a life that can be recommended to all those who follow you.

While the book is an excellent resource for personal reading and reflection, I believe it is also a good resource for discussion groups.

PREFACE

The design of this work is to stir to honorable effort those who are wasting their time and energies through indifference to life's prizes. In the furtherance of this aim the authors have endeavored to gather from all possible sources the thoughts of those wise and earnest men and women who have used their pens to delineate life and its possibilities, its joys and its sorrows. They do not claim to have furnished more than the setting in which are placed these "Gems" of thought. Their hope is that they may be able to awaken in the minds of the careless a sense of the value of life. To those who are striving nobly for true manhood or womanhood, they would bring words of encouragement. They trust that many may derive from its pages inspiration, which will serve to make real their hopes of success and happiness.

Cincinnati, January 1, 1880

*** In a few places, I have added comments or links to extra content that might be helpful. These are in *italics.*

****In keeping with the more formal writings of 1880, masculine pronouns are used to refer to mankind in general or sometimes to mean either a man or woman. Specific references to men or women are easily determined by the context.*

THE GIFT OF LIFE

The mind will never think more clearly than when contemplating a long, but misspent life. Standing near the end of life's journey, a person looks back over the years only to recall opportunities that passed by unimproved. He can plainly see where he hastily passed by the real "gems of life" in pursuit of the glittering attractions of pleasure which when gained turned to ashes in his very grasp. What a different course he would pursue if time could turn backwards and he were allowed to start again to weave the "tangled web of life." But this is not possible. Regrets are useless, except when they awaken in the minds of youth a wish to avoid errors and a desire to gather only the true "jewels of life."

Life is the choicest gift in the bounty of heaven committed to your wise and diligent keeping. But, beware! Its possibilities for woe are equal to those of success. God has given you existence, with full power and opportunity to improve it and be happy. He has also given you equal power to despise the gift and be miserable. Which you do is up to you. People mistakenly think they are mere creatures of fate. You may make life what you please and give it as much worth, both for yourself and others, as you desire.

Success in life is the development of the talents that God has given you. Every person carries within the key that unlocks either the door to success or failure. If you utterly fail, in the majority of cases, it is your own fault. You have either neglected to improve the talents God has given you, or you fail to enter the door that he has opened for you. If you have only one

11

talent, improve it. Don't neglect it just because you don't have ten.

Many of you today are just starting on this journey called life. Great destinies, responsibilities, dangers, and uncertainty lie hidden in the passages of everyday life. The future is like an unopened book. Even though you'd like to open it and see what's ahead, it is a task which only the hands of Time can accomplish.

Mankind everywhere desires to be successful—to make the most out of life. However, the path to success will not always be smooth and often lies amid rocks and cliffs, and not on lawns or among lilies. History and daily life are full of examples to show us that the measure of human achievements has always been proportional to the amount of human daring and doing. Therefore, meet life bravely.

Success may or may not be accompanied by wealth, position, and fame. It is in your power to live a life of integrity so that others will honor and respect you. You can speak words of encouragement to the downhearted, a kindly word of caution to the erring one. You can help remove some obstacle from the paths of the weak. You can incite in the minds of those around you a desire to live a pure life. You can urge those who are almost overwhelmed by sorrow, to look up and see the sunshine through the dark clouds passing over them. All this you can do, and a grand success you will be. In this sense, you only are to blame if you fail. Resolve to be in this truly successful. And then, if wealth or fame accompany you and others delight to give you honor, these will be just the frames encasing your true success.

As people get older and look back on their lives, they tend to have more regrets over what they didn't do vs. what they did do.

Todd Henry in his book, "Die Empty" told of a friend who asked a strange question in a meeting - "What do you think is the most valuable land in the world?" Several people guessed Manhattan, the oil fields of the Middle East, the gold mines of South Africa, etc. He then told the group, "You're all wrong. The most valuable land in the world is the graveyard. In the graveyard are buried all the unwritten novels, never-launched businesses, unreconciled relationships, and all the other things people thought, 'I'll get around to that tomorrow.' One day, however, their tomorrows ran out."

We need to share with our children and grandchildren lessons learned from our own life. Hopefully, they will have the wisdom to take heed and avoid their own regrets.

THE AIM OF LIFE

Without an aim of life, without a sail to propel, or rudder to guide you, the strong winds and currents of the world will sweep you this way and that. If you are not quickly wrecked or run aground, it is more your good fortune than good management.

Take heed of an aimless life. Take heed, also, of a low aim. However, having high standards and wishing to reach them, without any further effort on your part, is not enough to elevate you to any great degree. More than magnificent dreams are necessary for success in life. It is vain to hope for good results from mere plans. You will get the best results in every area of life when hard work follows your plans. A purpose without work is dead. But if you work without a purpose, you'll waste your efforts in a maze of inconsistencies.

To live life with purpose is a privilege no matter what the cost of transient pain and relentless toil. Live for something worthy of life and its opportunities. If some worthy purpose is kept in view, and effort is made every day of your life toward its accomplishment, you will achieve your goal. Everyone should have a goal in view and pursue it steadily. You should not be turned from your course by other attractive objects. Live for something definite and practical. Take hold of things with a will, and they will yield to you and become the mediators of your own and other's happiness.

Life is short, and yet it may be long enough for you to lose your character or your fortune. On the other hand, with diligence you can accomplish much within its limits. Life is not long enough for any one person to accomplish everything. However, any person endowed with ordinary intellect can accomplish at least one useful, important, and worthy purpose.

Have you ever considered what you are best capable of doing in this world? If not, put it off no longer. Determine to make the most of the powers and talents that God has given you and seize upon every outward advantage within your reach. A choice of business or occupation should be made with wise consideration of your capability and preference. You should be educated for it, and when this is done, pursue it with industry and enthusiasm that will warrant success. Live life as though the world had waited for your coming.

If a change of business is desired, be sure the fault is with the business and not yourself. For running here and there often leads to poverty when the sands of life are half run. Always remember that it is not your trade or profession that makes you respectable. It is simply an instrument put into your hands by which to gain for yourself and your loved ones the means of living until sickness or old age robs you of life.

There are some that make pleasure the aim of their lives—living only for their own enjoyment. Anyone, even a person who is totally independent and heir to millions, will certainly become a worthless character if he does not aim at something higher than his own selfish enjoyment. No person should live chiefly for his own selfish good. We promote our own happiness in the exact proportions we contribute to the comfort and happiness of others. In our strivings for "something better than we have known" we should work for others' good rather than our own pleasure. Those whose object in life is their own happiness find in the end that their lives are sad failures. A life thus spent is a life lost.

Work on human hearts and destinies to do imperishable work, to build within life's fleeting hours monuments that shall last forever. If such grand possibilities are within your reach, it's important that you live for *something* every hour of your existence. Yesterday was ours, but it is gone; tomorrow we may never see; *today* is all we possess. Therefore, in the golden hour of the present, seeds are planted which will yield a harvest of good or evil. What kind of seeds are you planting?

You should strive to attain a good character and set your aim so high that it will require years of patient toil to reach it. If you can reach it easily, it is unworthy of you. You must work as well as dream, labor as well as pray. Your hand must be as stout as your heart, your arm as strong as your head. *Purpose must be followed by action.* Then you are living and acting worthily of the great destinies that lay in store for you. Decide at once upon a noble purpose, then take it up bravely, bear it joyfully, and lay it down triumphantly.

I encourage you to listen to this recording entitled "The Strangest Secret" by Earl Nightingale before proceeding.

FAMILY LIFE

HOME

Home is a refuge—a place of rest and contentment—where the burdens of everyday life are relieved. No matter how humble the home may be, how destitute its reserves, or how poorly its family members may be clothed, you will find a friendly welcome from hearts beating true to your own. The chosen partner of your life's journey has a smile when others have deserted you, a hand of hope when all others refuse, and a heart to feel your sorrows. It should be the duty of all to make home so happy that you do not tire of it, but long for the hour when your day's toil is over because it is the happiest and dearest place on earth.

One danger of home life springs from its familiarity. Careless language and actions are apt to be indulged in when the eye of the world is shut out and the ear of the world cannot hear. At home our hearts wear no armor. Every arrow strikes them. Of all places on earth, home is the most delicate and sensitive. A single bitter word may disquiet the home for a whole day, but kind and gentle words and a sweet disposition will make the home peaceful and a place where happiness and blessing dwells.

It is in the home that we form many, if not most, of our habits. We carry these habits into the world. They cling to us. The vulgarities or grammatical blunders that we use at home are generally used in public. The home should be held too sacred to be polluted with vulgarities. The language of home should be chosen wisely so as to not stain the purest lips or fall harshly on the most refined ear.

In the great majority of cases it will be found that those who frequent bars and places of low resort do not have pleasant homes.

There are some people who apparently live more for the admiration of others than for those in their own household, and have a smile for all but those who should be the nearest and dearest. This will surely make a complete wreck of their own happiness and the home happiness.

Home has voices of experience and hearts of genuine love to instruct you in the way of life, and to save you from a sense of loneliness as you gradually discover the selfishness of mankind.

Home has its trials, which image the stern struggles of your later years, to strengthen your character and open the portals of your heart so that the jewels hidden there might shine forth and shed its luster on the world. Home has its duties, to teach you how to act responsibly. Home gradually increases its burdens so that you will acquire strength to endure without being overtasked. Home is a little world, in which the duties of the big world are rehearsed daily. It is in the home that we learn how to live life.

ADVICE TO PARENTS

Infancy is the morning of life. A great sense of responsibility fills the parents' hearts as they realize that in their hands and under their influence is to be molded a character. They are about to witness the unfolding of a human life.

The parents lay the foundation of a child's character. With what delicacy should they use the pencil of personal influence! The soul is soft, and the lines they make are deep and not easily erased. It is an immortal soul they work upon, and it will show forever some trace of their work. However trivial the influences which contribute to form the character of the child, they endure though life.

The things taught and modeled in the home influence character far more effectively than sermons, lectures, newspapers, and books. Parents should realize they are teachers and the foundation of our national life is in their hands. They can make it send forth waters bitter or sweet, for the death or the healing of the people. The smallest bit of opinion sown in the minds of children in the home emerge later to become the world's public opinions, for nations are gathered out of nurseries.

It is in childhood that the mind is most open to impression and ready to be kindled by the first spark that flies into it. The first joy, the first failure, the first achievement, the first misadventure, is always remembered by the child. Early impressions are not easily erased and endure to exert a great influence on our lives. The influence in the early days of childhood is often like the "casting of bread upon the waters"—often not found in any of its favorable developments until after "many days."

Influence is as quiet and imperceptible on the child's mind as falling snowflakes. In many instances secret and unnoticed influences have been in operation for months, even years, to break down the strongest barriers of the human heart, and work out its moral ruin while even the fondest parents and friends have been unaware of such unseen agents of evil.

By example, much more than by precept, children are taught to speak kindly to each other, to acknowledge favors, to be gentle and unselfish, to be thoughtful and considerate of others. So, if the father shows kindly attention to the mother, children will see the act and make note of it. Children are great imitators, and enjoy trying to do what they see other people do.

The influences of home perpetuate themselves. The gentle graces of the mother live on in the daughter long after her head is pillowed in death. The fatherly kindness echoes in the goodness and character of sons who come to wear his mantle and fill his place. On the other hand, from an unhappy, mismanaged home, go forth persons who will perpetuate the sorrows, sadness, and contentions that made their own early lives miserable.

Make your children helpful and useful, and you make them happy. Teach them early to form habits of neatness, and when you are weary you will not have to clean up after them because of their carelessness.

Parents must take an interest in their children, and draw them to their hearts. There is no mystery in attaching children to one's self. If you love them, they will love you. If you make much of them, they will make much of you. They have a quick way of discerning who really loves them and cares for them.

Parents do well to study the character of younger ones. The majority of parents do not understand their children. They are kept under restraint, and aren't properly developed. They live a life of fear rather than of love, which should not be. Have confidence in each other, and the seeds properly sown will spring forth with fruits that will bud and blossom.

It is a sad fact that few children confide in their parents. Do not be satisfied without some account of each day's joys and sorrows. Never think anything that affects the happiness of your children too small a matter to claim your attention. To the little child, home is his world—he knows no other. Home is the spot where the child pours out all his complaint, and it is the grave of all his sorrows. It is a source of great comfort to the innocent child to tell all troubles to mother or father, and they should lend a willing ear. Always send the little child to bed happy. No matter what cares may trouble your mind, give the little one a goodnight kiss as he or she goes to bed. The memory of this will inspire the heart with courage to face the stormy years that may be in store for it.

Parents do not realize how far a word of praise will go with children. Praise is sunshine to a child, and there is no child who does not need it. Praise spurs a child on to earnest effort. It is the high reward of one's struggle to do right. When children perform little acts of kindness for their elders, parents should show their appreciation or the habit is soon dropped. Many a child, starving for the praise that parents should give, runs off eagerly after the flattery of others. To withhold praise where it is due is dishonest and often leaves a stinging sense of injustice—especially in children. One may as well think to grow flowers in frost as to think of raising children successfully with rebuke and constant criticism.

When it becomes necessary to reprove children, be careful to do it with kindness and gentleness. The effect will be much better. Hearts of children are much like flowers; they remain open to the softly falling dew, but close in the violent downfall of rain. Never reprove children before strangers, for children are sensitive, and wish strangers to think well of them. Blame, when administered before visitors, takes away the motivation for doing well.

The law of love is great, but it shows its full strength when united with kindness. There is a magic power in gentle words, the potency of which only a few people are able to resist. In the home governed by the spirit of love, each one strives to avoid giving offense, and is considerate of the others' happiness.

Sometimes angry and hasty words pass between father and mother or brother and sister. To judge from their actions, they do not appear to love each other. It doesn't seem to occur to them that it is their duty, as it ought to be their pleasure, to do and say all that they possibly can for each other's good and happiness.

If you want your home to be a cheerful spot where happiness and peace may be found, then don't let loud, harsh words be uttered within its walls. The husband and wife should speak gently to one another. Speak gently to the wayward child. A hasty word is of consequence. Parents must be careful to guard their lips and banish all cross words and impatient gestures. Let only kind and loving tones fall on children's ears. The little things they see and hear about them mold them for eternity. Observe how quick the child's eye is to perceive the meaning of looks, voices, and motions. A pleasant smile and a word of kindness will often restore good humor and playfulness.

The remembrance of an unkind word brings with it a bitter sting. Speak gently to the erring one; are we not all weak and liable to err? Temptation that we don't know about may have surrounded him. Harshness will drive him on the sinful way; gentleness may win him back to virtue.

The home in which true courtesy and politeness reigns is a home from which polite men and women go forth. Any ingrained virtue exhibits itself first at home. Children should be trained to behave at home, as you would have them behave when outside the home. It is the home life that is acted out when they are away. In the actions of children, strangers can read a history of the home life. Teach them to give you courteous speech and manners and they will live to honor you.

In homes where true courtesy prevails it seems to meet you on the threshold. You feel the kindly welcome on entering. The delightful atmosphere that pervades the house is unmistakable. No angry voices are heard upstairs. No sullen children are sent to their room.

Family members lose nothing by mutual politeness. The goodnight and the good-morning salutation, though they seem trivial, have a sweet and softening influence on all. Something is wrong in those homes where the little courtesies of speech are ignored.

When the family gathers around the breakfast or dinner table, the same courtesy should prevail as if guests were present. Reproof, complaint, unpleasant discussions, sarcasm, and moody silence should be banished. Reproofs from parents have their time and place, but should never intrude upon the social life of the family and make the home uncomfortable. A serious word in private will generally cure a fault more easily than many public criticisms. In some families a spirit of contradiction mars the harmony. Every statement is dissected and the absolute correctness of every word calculated. It interferes with social freedom when unimportant inaccuracies are watched for and exposed for the sake of exposure.

It is the duty of parents to make their homes the most pleasant spot on earth for their children and their friends. They should make it so attractive that it will not only firmly hold its own loved ones, but will draw others into the home also. Go to great lengths to provide amusements, which if not provided at home, would entice them elsewhere. You are far better off to spend your money doing this than to amass a fortune for your children to spend in the future. The richest legacy you can leave your child is a life-long memory of a pleasant home. Children raised in such homes will leave them with regret and look forward to coming back to them.

Not all the appliances that wealth can buy are necessary for a happy childhood. Homes are not made up of material things. It is not a big house, rich furniture, and a luxurious table that make a home. Too frequently the effect of prosperity renders the heart cold and selfish, but the heart will never forget the influence of a happy home. Happy home memories will be an evening of enjoyment to which the lapse of years will only add new sweetness. Such a home memory is a constant inspiration for good, and a constant restraint from evil.

Many a child goes astray, not because there is a lack of prayers or virtue at home, but simply because the home lacks sunshine. You should always try to make the home cheerful and synonymous with happiness. Far too many homes are like the frame of a harp that stands without strings. In form and outline they suggest music, but no melody arises from the empty spaces. Such a home is unattractive, dreary and dull. Among home amusements, the best is the good old habit of conversation. Conversation is the sunshine of the mind.

Cultivate singing in the family. Teach the songs and hymns of your childhood to your own little ones. The home songs not only serve to make the present home life happy and agreeable, but the very memory of it will serve as a shield of defense in times of trial and temptation.

The home is the nursery of affection. It is the heart's garden where seeds of love should be planted and carefully tended. They should be guarded against the frosts of jealousy, anger, envy, pride, vanity, and ambition. It is around the memories of home that cluster the happiest and sometimes the saddest recollections of youth.

The wisest parents have forethought enough to provide not only for the youth but also for the age of their offspring. They teach them usefulness, and not to expect too much from the world; to become familiar with the stern and actual realities of life, and never to be apes of fashion or parasites of greatness. Parents should educate their children not merely in scholastic acquirements, but in the knowledge of the respective positions they are to occupy when they become men and women. Educate the girl in the intricate duties that will be required of her as a wife and mother, and that it rests with herself whether it shall be exalted or whether it shall be debased and lowly. Educate the boy to the knowledge of what the busy world will require of him.

It must be remembered that the most important part of the education of children, whether for good or evil, is carried on at home, often unconsciously in their amusements, and under the daily influence of what they see and hear about them. They must be taught to exercise all their senses to choose good and refuse evil.

Teach children that they lead two lives, the life without and the life within; that the inside must be pure in the sight of God, as well as the outside in the sight of man.

What is more beautiful than the eyes of a child—clear wells of undefiled thought? Full of hope, love and curiosity, they meet your own. Children make us tender and sympathetic, and a thousand times reward us for all we do for them. We are indebted to them for constant incentives to noble living and a perpetual reminder that we do not live for ourselves alone. We owe them gratitude for the dark hour their presence has brightened; for their helplessness and dependence which have won us from ourselves; for their kisses placed on brows that if not for their caressing would be wrinkled into frowns. They create sport and amusement and banish all sense of loneliness from the household. But children grow up; nothing on earth grows so fast as children. The house will soon enough not have a child left in it. There is no more noise in the house. It is more orderly now. There are no more toys, games, bats, balls, or dolls scattered about to litter the best room. There are no longer any tasks before you lie down. But the mother's heart is heavy, and the father's house is lonely.

ADVICE TO CHILDREN

Think of the helplessness of infancy, the dependence of childhood, the necessities and wants of youth, the long years of unwearied toil of parents—and then say whether it is possible for children to repay too much love and gratitude to their parents. What thankfulness should fill every child's heart! Every day you should give your parents some token of love.

The time will come, if it has not already, when you must part from those who have surrounded you in childhood. The new relationships you form and the business you pursue may call you far from the "play-place" of your youth.

There is a liability when a son or daughter leaves the home of their childhood and forms a home of their own that they will lose their old attachments and cease to pay attention to parents. New associations, new thoughts, new cares come in, and if special effort isn't taken, they crowd out the old love. *This ought never to be.* Children should remember that the change is in them and not with those they left behind. They have everything that is new, but the parents' hearts cling to the past. When children go away, they don't know or understand what it cost to give them up or the vacancy they left behind and they never will until they experience it themselves. Many times the parents don't have, as the children do, any new loves to take the place of the old.

If you live close to your parents, be sure to frequently visit them. Even when many miles away, make it a priority to go to your parents. In this matter do not regard time or expense. They are well spent. Some day when the word reaches you that your father or mother is gone, you will not regret the many hours of travel spent in going to them while they were yet alive.

Nothing better recommends an individual than his attention to his parents. There are some children who watch over their parents, supply all their wants, and by their devotion and kindness remove all care and sorrow from their parent's hearts. On the other hand, there are others who never seem to even think of their parents, and care little whether they are comfortably situated or not. By their conduct they increase their parents' cares, embitter their lives, and bring their gray hairs with sorrow down to the grave. Others, by sin and vice, have drained their parents' cup of happiness and made them anxious for death to release them from their sufferings.

You may disappoint the ambition of your parents. You may be unable to distinguish yourself as you hoped, but let it not deter you from being a son or daughter whose moral character they need ever to be ashamed.

There is no period of life when our parents do not need our attention and love. It should be our constant study how we can best promote their welfare and happiness, and smooth the pillow of their declining years. When called away from our presence, which sooner or later must happen, the thought will be sweet that they departed in comfort and peace. However, if we denied them what their circumstances and necessities required, our remorse will prove a thorn in our flesh, piercing us sharply, and filling our days with regret.

The duties of children to their parents are considered far too little. As the children grow up, parents depend on them much earlier than either imagine. Determine to be a staff your parents can lean on in their declining years. It is not sufficient to simply give them a home to make their declining years comfortable. While supplying their physical wants, their hearts may be yearning for some expression of love from you. If you think they have outgrown these desires, you are mistaken.

Can you begrudge a few extra steps for the mother who never stopped to number those you demanded during your helpless infancy? Have you the heart to slight her requests or treat her remarks with indifference when you cannot begin to measure the patient devotion with which she bore your peculiarities? Anticipate her wants, express your affections as heartily as you did when a child, so that she may never have occasion to grieve in secret for the child she has lost. Every little attention you can show your mother brings back the youth of her heart and fills it with pleasure and happiness.

Neither is the father wholly indifferent to expressions of devoted love. He may pretend to care little for them, but it would give him pain if they were entirely withheld. Fathers and mothers need their children just as much as their children need them.

Keep in touch with your parents. Do not believe that to them "no news is good news." Write or call them, even if it is only to say, "I love you." These messages will be like jewels, and the tears that fall fondly over them will be treasures for you.

LOVE LIFE

Love in one form or another is the ruling element of life. Love of dominion or power, though utterly selfish in its aims and methods, has been many times marvelously overruled for good in the world's history. The love of knowledge, in the pursuit of which lives have been lost and fortunes spent, has resulted in the discovery of secrets that have contributed much for the advancement of the human race. But the love that is grander than any other is that indescribable, ever fresh and beautiful love between a man and a woman. That love finds a man rough, uncultivated, and selfish and makes him a refined and courteous gentleman. It transforms the timid, bashful girl into a woman of matchless power for good.

Love is an actual need, an urgent requirement of the heart. Every human being feels a necessity of loving and being loved. As a woman is not a woman until she has known love, neither is man a complete man.

Genuine love is founded on appreciation and respect. The most beautiful may be the most admired and caressed, but they are not always the most valued and loved. We may discover great beauty in those who are not beautiful if they possess genuine truthfulness, simplicity, and sincerity.

Love is a tender plant and cannot bear cold neglect. It requires kind acts and thoughtful attention to one another. Love purifies the heart from self. It is the triumph of the unselfish over the selfish part of our nature. It strengthens the character and gives higher motives to every action of life. The way of selfishness is self-seeking; that of love, self-sacrifice.

Love blends young hearts in blissful unity and ignores past ties and affections so as to make a son willing to separate from his father's house, and the daughter from all the sweet endearments of her childhood home.

The love of a woman is a stronger power and a sweeter thing than that of a man because she sacrifices more. Men and women cannot be judged by the same rules. Man is a creature of interest and ambition. His nature leads him into the struggle and bustle of the great world. He seeks for fame, fortune, and space in the world's thoughts. But a woman's heart is her world. It is there her ambition strives for empire. It is there her nature seeks for love and kindness. For every woman, love is the food of the heart and it's possible to exist on a very small quantity, but this small quantity is an absolute necessity.

The bosom that does not feel love is cold; the mind that does not conceive it is dull; the philosophy that does not accept it is false; and the only true religion in the world has pure, reciprocal, and undying love for its basis.

COURTSHIP

In the questions of love, courtship and marriage, it is to be deeply regretted that men and women do not more carefully consider the wisdom of their course and reflect whether they are guided by the light of calm, clear-headed sense or impulse. They shouldn't trust too much the impulse of the heart or be too easily captivated by a winning exterior. Discretion tempers passion, and it is precisely this quality more than any other that is found to be absent in courtship.

Sadly, it has been said that years are necessary to cement a friendship while months, sometimes weeks, or even days are sufficient to prepare for marriage. Whether as a matter of convenience or for the mere purpose of securing a home and being settled in life, thousands enter into the most sacred of human relationships unprepared to bear the burdens that it brings.

Courtship love should be to marital love what a blossom is to the perfected fruit. The power of this love must be measured, not by its intensity, but by its effects. Not once in a hundred times do two natures brought side by side harmonize in every part. Very rich and fruitful natures are often side-by-side with barren ones; sensitive, with those coarse and rude. This is a consequence of the lack of thought by people who are about to marry.

True wisdom will say to the young, "Love, but love not blindly." Justice is represented as blind, so that under no circumstance, can she be accused of personal favor or prejudice. Love on the other hand, should use her eyes to the fullest extent so that in the days of courtship, no stumbling block may be left to become a torment after marriage.

All young men and women should decide with the aid of others' experience, with calm and careful consideration, and with an appeal for guidance from on high, if the person he or she proposes to unite their destiny to is the one with whom they are best suited to make the journey. If, as a result of such reflection, they are convinced that the choice is wise, they may confidently proceed to take upon themselves the duties and privileges of marriage. But if such observation shows that they have erred, as they value their future happiness and the happiness of others, let them stop before the vow is made that unites their fate with another's.

Courtship in the life of a woman is a garden where no weeds mingle with the flowers, and all is lovely and beautiful. Courtship is the first turning point in the life of a woman, crowded with perils and temptation. The rose tints of affection dazzle and bewilder the imagination, and while always bearing in mind that life without love is a wilderness, it should not be overlooked that true affection requires solid support.

The object of courtship is not to woo, charm, gratify, or please, simply for the present pleasure. It is for the selection of a life companion—one who must bear, suffer, and enjoy life with us in its frowns as well as smiles, in its joys as well as sorrows—one who will walk pleasantly, willingly, and confidingly by our side through all of life.

Seek a companion who would approve what you approve and condemn what you condemn, not for the purpose of agreeing with you, but of his or her own free will. It is one who, when given a combination of circumstances, would be affected, feel, and act as you would. Courtship then is a voyage of discovery established by mutual consent of two people to see to what extent there is harmony existing between them.

The man should seek a true companion who does not parade herself around as store goods. She has a pure, loving heart and good common sense that are far more valuable than personal beauty or wealth. No sacrifice she can make is too great, no adversity so stern that it can shake her resolve or hopefulness. Such a woman is a partner as God designed a wife to be.

Can you reveal to her the sacred treasures of your mind, which lie hidden from the careless gaze of others, and be assured of her sympathy? Can she walk hand in hand with you as your equal, honored above all women? Can she sit in your household as a shining light, respected for her gentle dignity and the wisdom of her management and conversation? It is in error, which has proved fatal to many young lives, to marry one whom you consider your inferior in heart or mind. A wife has the power to make or destroy the home, so a man must ponder these questions.

It is equally fatal for a woman to marry a man who is her inferior. She of necessity descends to his level. Being his superior in every good sense of the word, she cannot have for him that high feeling of regard that every wife should have for her husband. Lacking that, love soon fades away, and only the duties of married life remain; its pleasures are all gone. Young men inclined to uncontrolled habits do not have sufficient moral stamina to enable them to resist temptation and are consequently deficient in self-respect. Such a man cannot rightly appreciate the tender and loving nature of a true woman. What is wanted in both is a true companion; not one who possesses wealth, not necessarily the possessor of a scholastic education, but one who has a pure, warm heart and good common sense.

MARRIED LIFE

In the minds of nearly every person and in accordance to the desires that God has put into our physical being, there exists the hope and expectation of marriage. Therefore, it is proper to prepare for marriage since it is designed by our Creator to promote happiness, health, and purity.

Marriage has a great refining and moralizing tendency. When a man marries early and uses prudence in choosing a suitable companion, he is likely to lead a virtuous and happy life. In an unmarried state all alluring vices have a tendency to draw him away. While there are exceptions to every rule, the chances are that the young man who marries will make a stronger and better fight all through life than if he remains single. A single man may have a place to eat, a place to sleep and all the luxury that money can buy, but money will not buy everything. It is utterly beyond its power to purchase the treasures of true love.

Marriage, to be a blessing, must be properly entered. It has its fundamental laws which must be obeyed. The reasons for every enjoyment of married life may be understood before entering the relationship. Therefore, every youth, both male and female, should make marriage a study. It should not be entered blindly, in total ignorance of what it is and what its conditions for happiness are. The marriage relationship involves some of the most stern duties and acts of self-denial that a man or woman is called on to perform.

For all professions and trades in life, men and women prepare themselves by studying and devoting time and money to learn the general principles and duties of the trade or profession. Marriage, the most important and holy relationship of life, should be entered upon with the same due diligence.

Every couple flatters themselves that their experience will be better than the many that have gone before them. They look with amazement at the coldness, complaining and dissatisfaction that spoil so many homes as things that cannot possibly affect them. But, to avoid the misfortunes of others, they must avoid their mistakes.

It is so easy to imagine that the one you love is perfect. Courtship is to many a dreamy place between the joys of youth and the cares of marriage. The dreams of courtship vanish into thin air soon after the wedding ring is put on. No ceremony can change a person's nature. Young people seldom expose their defects when courting. They are apt to marry faultless. Love is blind, but faults are there and will come out. The joys of the wedding day and honeymoon are quickly followed by the duties and anxious cares of daily life. This is the trying time of married life. There can be no more illusions between husband and wife. The deceptions of courtship become apparent.

Many young couples discover character traits in each other that astonishes them. Everyday may reveal something new and possibly something unpleasant. The courtship character slowly fades away and too often the courtship love as well. Now come disappointment, sorrow, and regret. They also awaken to the fact that married life is full of cares and disappointments. This should have been expected, but under the light of hope, couples have a tendency to see only joys in their future. If only every couple would consider that over against every joy stands a disappointment, and that tears and smiles alternate with each other through life, they would save themselves much disappointment. Trials and sufferings are tests that bring out the real character, and ultimately can bring husband and wife closer together. When two people with affectionate and sensible natures recognize this, the result can be the closest of unions.

Our everyday wants and desires remain the same after as before marriage. The marriage ceremony does not do away with the necessity of self-control. Passions still have to be subdued and a careful watch maintained against hasty words and actions. Many, in failing to recognize this, are laying a foundation for future unhappiness.

We have all seen a tree die in the summertime. But the tree doesn't die all at once. First, a leaf sickens here and there and fades. Next, a whole branch feels the touch of coming death. Finally, the feeble signs of sickly life, visible here and there, all disappear and the dead trunk holds outs its stripped limbs in melancholy ruin. In the same way, wedded love sometimes dies. Wedded love, blessed with the prayers of friends, hallowed by the sanction of God, rosy with present joys, and radiant with future hope, doesn't die all at once. A hasty word casts a shadow upon it and then the shadow deepens with a sharp reply. A little thoughtlessness misconstrued, a little unintentional negligence deemed real, a little word misinterpreted allows sorrow and dissension to enter the family circle and eventually nothing remains of the union but the legal form—the dead trunk of the tree.

The plain rules of courtesy, kindness, consideration, and respect are as necessary now as in the springtime of love. A spirit of courtesy should constantly exist between husband and wife. Before marriage each would be cautious of breaking manners. Is not courtesy just as important now? Has the marriage ceremony given you any right to be less than polite?

Marriage offers the most effective opportunity for spoiling the life of another. Nobody can debase, harass, and ruin a woman as her own husband, and nobody can do as much to chill a man's aspirations or paralyze his energies as his wife. Have you seriously considered that each of you has the power to make the other utterly miserable?

The man or woman who wants to conveniently blame the ills of married life on marrying the wrong person ought to look in the mirror for the cause of their trouble. They are usually accustomed to thinking of happiness for themselves as the chief end of marriage. No magic of "matchmaking" would make the lives of such people perfect. A good marriage requires thoughtfulness, self-control, consideration for others, patience and other qualities without which life is unendurable in any relationship. Nowhere does it prove so powerfully true as in married life that your happiness is found in consulting the happiness of another. Marriage is a school for the exercise of virtue, and is the source and nurturer of many of the best qualities in the life of a man or woman.

Husbands and wives should learn to live together happily, for the lesson *can* be learned. By living happily together we do not mean a calm, passive existence unbroken by a single dissenting word or look. Occasional differences of opinion indicate mutual vitality. But in all *vital* points of mutual interest husband and wife should agree perfectly, understanding that in every sense of the word they are one.

You have one life to live, and no amount of money or influence or fame can compensate you for a life of unhappiness. You cannot afford to quarrel with each other. You cannot afford to cherish a single thought, to harbor a single desire, to gratify a single passion, or indulge a single selfish feeling, that will tend to make this union anything but a source of happiness to you. Therefore, resolve that you will be happy together and that if you suffer it shall be from the same cause and in perfect sympathy. It is not too late for you to look for happiness. It is folly to expect only disappointment the rest of your life.

Human character, by wise Providence, is infinitely varied, and there are not two individuals in existence so entirely alike in their tastes, habits of thought, and natural aptitude that they can keep step with one another over all the rough places in the journey of life. There must be leaning on one another. The compromise cannot be all on one side. You can be happy together, but the agreement to be happy must be mutual. A good marriage is the result of years of mutual endeavor to please, and comes with patient efforts to learn each other's disposition and taste. Draw your souls closer and closer together from year to year.

The great secret is to learn to bear with each other's failings and not be blind to them. We are to hide them from the curious gaze of others and not let them chill the affections.

If you observe faults in your companion, keep them to yourself. What right do you have to inform others of their presence? Neither father nor mother, brother nor sister has any right to be informed of the secrets of your married life. A husband and wife have no business telling one another's faults to anybody but themselves. In all public places and among friends, refer to one another with consideration and respect.

We believe two things are essential to the happiness of married life—to have a home of your own and to live honestly within your means. A great proportion of the failures in marriage can be traced directly to the neglect of the latter rule. A clear understanding of income and expenses is necessary for peace in every home.

To regulate your expenses by other people's income is the height of folly and to contract debts for a style of living that is of your neighbor's choosing rather than your own is akin to insanity. And when you reflect on how needless this is, you can readily see that in this instance, as in many others, the trials are of our own choosing, and might be avoided by consideration and care. No sensible person will consider it a hardship to begin on a moderate scale. Those who begin this way and afterwards attain wealth always look back on the days of "small things" with peculiar satisfaction as among the happiest of their life.

A great deal has been said in a cynical way about the number of unhappy marriages. It is easy to forget that for every instance of complaint there are many happy and prosperous unions of which the world never hears. Men and women whose married life is full of good don't often feel the need to defend the system under which they live.

The institution of marriage is the bond of social order, and if treated with due respect, care, and consideration, greatly enhances individual happiness and consequently the general good. For ages, history has shown that the permanent union of one man with one woman establishes a relationship of affection and interest that can in no other way be made to exist between two human beings.

~≈ ⚘ ≈~

ADVICE TO HUSBANDS

You who have taken a wife from a happy home, have you done what you could to make amends for the loss of her friends and companions? Always remember that you chose her because you considered her superior to all others. She was young and cherished by her parents and siblings. She left everyone and everything she has depended on for comfort, affection, kindness and pleasure—turning with joyful anticipation of happiness yet to come. She left all to join her destiny with yours—to make your home happy, and to do all that she could to meet your wishes, and to lighten the burdens that might press upon you. Therefore, take care to not blast such hopes and destroy the confidence which your love inspired!

It is no less true now than in the morning of time that it is "not good for man to be alone." All through life, through storms and sunshine, conflicts and victory, a man needs a woman's love. Let him also return this love. There are husbands so cold and formal that they have no kiss or caress for the wives whom they really love. There are wives to whom a single demonstration would tell their hearts how fondly they are loved, and would be better than untold riches.

Who can estimate the value of a woman's affections? In a good wife the husband finds not only affection, but also companionship—a companionship with which no other can compare. The treasure of a wife's affection, like the grace of God, is given, not bought. Gold cannot purchase a gem so precious. Money can cut down forests, build houses, cities and roads, but it cannot purchase true love and the affection of a wife. If any husband has failed to appreciate the affections of his wife, he will surely realize the value when the heart that loved him is stilled by death.

The husband should have as his goal and rule of conduct the happiness of his wife. His affection should show itself not in caresses alone, but in that he also consults the judgment as well as the wishes of his wife. He will find in her his best counselor; for her instincts will usually lead him right, where his own unaided reason might go wrong.

We exhort you who are a husband to love your wife even as you love yourself. Continue through life with the same tenderness that in youth gained her affections. Devote yourself to her and highly prize her company. Your wife wishes to feel that she is precious to you—not useful, not valuable, not convenient, but that she is dear to you. Let her be the recipient of your polite and wholehearted attentions. Let her see that her cares and loves are noticed, appreciated, and returned, her opinions asked, her approval sought, and her judgment respected. In short, let her *only* be loved, honored, and cherished in fulfillment of the marriage vow, and she will be a wellspring of pleasure to you.

ADVICE TO WIVES

A man's moral character is powerfully influenced by his wife. A lower nature will drag him down, as a higher one will lift him up. A woman of high principle will elevate the aim and purpose of her husband, just as one of low principle will degrade them. In the course of life we may see even a weak man display real public virtue because he had by his side a woman of noble character. Thus a wife may be the making or unmaking of the best of men. A good wife is constantly exerting influence for the good of her husband. She is the wielder of the moral pruning knife—constantly snipping off from her husband's moral nature little things that are growing in the wrong direction.

Many a man who has risen from obscurity to fame has acknowledged that he owed much of his success to the encouragement of his wife. The powers and influence of a good wife are immense. A good wife is to a man wisdom and courage, strength and endurance. She is a staff to lean on in time of trial and difficulty, and she is never lacking in sympathy and solace when distress occurs or fortune frowns.

We exhort you who are a wife to let your employment and pleasures be in the home.

Let your husband see that you really have a strong desire to make him happy. Enter into all his plans with interest. Sweeten all his troubles with your sympathy. Make him feel that there is always one ear that will listen, one heart that understands him, one refuge for him in all circumstances, and one warm, soft pillow for his head, beneath which a heart is beating with affection.

MANHOOD

Each age has its peculiar duties, privileges, pleasures and pains. When young we trust ourselves too much; when old we trust others too little. Rashness is the error of youth, and timid caution is the error of age. In youth we plan for ourselves a course of action through life. But as we approach old age we see more and more plainly how little control we really had in the course of our life. In childhood a lifetime seems an endless period. At manhood we are surprised that time goes by so rapidly and we start to comprehend the fleeting period of life. In old age the years that are passed seem as a dream of the night, our life as a tale nearly told. Childhood is the season of dreams and high resolves; manhood, of plans and actions; age, of retrospection and either satisfaction or regret.

There is certainly no age with more potential for good or evil than that of early manhood. It is the season of life when a man catches the first glimpse of the possibilities in store for him. What higher aim can he propose to himself than to become a man who lives not only for time but also for eternity? Every young man should be determined to do all the good he can, and to leave the world a better place for his having lived in it. A young man ought to be prepared to fill with honor and usefulness the places that he is destined to occupy. Beautiful lives have sometimes blossomed in the darkest and most unsuspected places. Pure, white lilies, full of fragrance, sometimes bloom on slimy, stagnant waters.

The cause of truth and virtue calls for champions, and the field for doing good is white unto the harvest. If a man enlists in the ranks and his spirit faints not, he may write his name among the stars of heaven.

Wealth, birth, and official station may secure an external, superficial courtesy, but they never did and never will secure the reverence of the heart. It is only the man who blends a cultivated mind with an upright heart that secures a deep and genuine respect.

If any are ambitious to possess true manhood, they will be men of reflection who recognize that life is a real and earnest affair and who fully realize the importance of every step they take and bring to it the careful consideration of a trained mind. The man who reads, studies, and meditates has intelligence stamped on his brow and gleaming in his eye. There are some who, though they are done growing, are only boys. They lack the ability to observe, examine, reason, and execute—in short, the ability to think. They don't have the ability to look beyond the present.

As we often mistake glittering tinsel for solid gold, so we often mistake appearances for true worth and manhood. We are too prone to take professions and words in lieu of actions; too easily impressed with nice clothes and polite manners to inquire into the character and doings of the individual. Man should be rated, not by his hoards of gold or by the temporary influence he may for a time exert, but by the unwavering principles that shape his character and his life. His fortress is wisdom. He is governed always by just principles and the highest motives in doing good. These constitute his only true manliness.

~~⚜~~

WOMANHOOD

Many women do the work of their life without being seen or noticed by the world. The world sees a family reared to virtue, one child after another growing into Christian manhood or womanhood, and at last sees them gathered around the grave where the mother that bore them rests from her labors. But the world never sees the quiet woman laboring for her children, providing them meals, teaching them prayers, and making their homes comfortable and happy.

A woman's happiness flows to her from sources and through channels different from those that bring happiness to a man. Her powers are eminently practical. She has a rich store of practical good sense, an ample fund of tact, skill, shrewdness, inventiveness, and management. It is her work to form the young mind, to give it direction and instruction, to develop its love for the good and true. It is her work to make the home happy, to nourish and instill all the virtues which make men and women good citizens. She soothes the sorrows of childhood, and ministers to the poor and distressed.

A woman's influence flows from her sensibilities, her gentleness, and her tenderness. It is these that disarm prejudice, and awaken confidence and affection in all who come within her sphere, and make her more powerful to accomplish her will than if nature had endowed her with the strength of a giant. As a wife and mother, she is seen in her most sacred and dignified aspect. As such she has great influence over the character of individuals, the condition of families, and therefore, the destiny of empires.

A good woman never grows old. When we look at a good woman we never think of her age because benevolence and virtue dwell in her heart and she looks as happy as she did in the springtime of life. In her neighborhood she is a friend and benefactor; in the Church, a devout worshiper and exemplary Christian. Who does not love and respect the woman who has spent her days in acts of kindness and mercy? If a young lady desires to retain the bloom and beauty of youth, let her not yield to the way of fashion and folly, but let her love truth and virtue.

A true woman exists independent of outward adornments. It is not wealth, beauty, connections, station, intelligence, or outward accomplishments that make the woman. These often adorn womanhood as the ivy adorns the oak, but they shouldn't be mistaken for the one they adorn. The great error of womankind is that they take the shadow for the substance, the glitter for the gold, and the trappings of the world for the priceless essence of real worth that exists in the mind and in the heart.

Women do not desire to be worshipped like an idol, but what is most acceptable to the heart of a woman is courtesy and just appreciation of her proper position, merit, and character. A woman surpasses a man in the quickness of her perception and in the right direction of her sympathies.

The moral worth of a woman holds a man in restraint and preserves his ways from becoming utterly corrupt. Mighty is the power of a woman in this respect. Even with all our churches, ministers, Bibles and sermons, man would be a prodigal without the restraint of a woman's virtue. Women first lay their hands on our young faces, plant the first seeds and make the first impressions. Every virtue of a woman has its influence on the world. A brother, husband, friend, or son is touched by its sunshine. Every prayer she breathes is answered, to some degree, in the hearts and lives of those she loves.

It is to be regretted that every young woman doesn't have a set purpose of life—some grand aim. Every young woman should also determine to do something for the honor and elevation of her sex. Her powers of mind and body should be applied to a good end. In every class of society the young women should awaken to their duty. They have a great work to do. It is not enough that they should be what their mothers were—they must be more. Will they heed the call?

A woman's influence is the chief anchor of society. No costly marble can build a more beautiful monument to her memory than the impression she makes on her own household. The honest example of a true mother reigns *queen* in the hearts of her children forever. She molds their minds and is the author of their grandest achievements. Cruelty she despises, and it lessens at her bidding; purity she admires, and it grows in her presence; music she loves, and her home is full of its melody; happiness is her herald, and she infuses the world with a desire for enjoyment. The world is moved and civilization is advanced by the silent influence of women. Man may make his monument of granite or marble, woman makes hers of immortality.

VIRTUES TO ACQUIRE

DIGNITY OF WORK

Without labor nothing can be accomplished. It is most fitting that man should not taste life's greatest happiness or reach the summit of his ambition without long and patient labor.

God in his wisdom has ordained that life shall be a scene of labor. Someone has said, "Nature holds for each of us all that we need to make us useful and happy; but she requires us to labor for all that we get." We can expect to overcome difficulties only by strong and determined efforts.

The secret to success or failure is usually contained in the answer to the question, "How earnest are you?" If you wish to succeed, you must do as you would to get through a crowd to a gate all are anxious to reach—hold your ground and push hard; to stand still is to give up ground in the battle.

As a young person catches the first light of a dream, and then looks down the long and narrow path by which others have reached it, he is likely to be disgusted with the passage and seek success through broader and quicker channels. It is here that young men and women have shipwrecked their lives. There is no easy road to success. The path passes through troubles and discouragements, through fields of earnest, patient labor. It is hard work, step by step, that secures success. While energy and perseverance are securing the prize for steady workers, others, sitting down by the wayside, are wondering why they cannot also be successful. They forget that work is the key.

Let none feel a sense of disappointment that life to them becomes routine. The same wants, the same demands, and similar duties meet us on the threshold of every day. We look forward to some great occasion when we can give proof of a heroic spirit, while complaining about the petty routine of daily life. On the contrary, it is this succession of little duties apparently of no account, which constitute the grand work of life.

Regardless of a person's natural gifts, he or she cannot expect to attain a high level of success in any profession without going through a vast amount of work which many would call drudgery. That quality which many call genius is not the ability to get along without work, but, on the contrary, is generally the capacity of doing an immense amount of work. The most illustrious names in history were hard workers. No one whom posterity delights to honor ever dreamed or idled his or her way to fame. To be idle and useless is neither an honor nor a privilege. Always make yourself useful, regardless of your position and economic status.

Young people ought to judge the dignity of labor by its usefulness and not by the gloss it wears. All honest work is honorable; and if your occupation is not as high-sounding as you would like, it is still better to work faithfully at this until opportunity opens the door to something higher. Regard labor as honorable, and dignify the task before you no matter what it is. Exalt your adopted calling or profession. Never allow depreciation of your work, no matter what it is. Whatever you try to do in life, try with all your heart to do it well without thought of fame or fortune. Whatever you devote yourself to, devote yourself to it completely.

It is not work, but overwork, that is hurtful. It is not hard work, but monotonous, hopeless work that is detrimental. All hopeful work is healthful, and to be usefully employed is one of the great secrets of happiness. The man or woman who has not learned to work doesn't know the thrill or pleasure experienced by one who carries a difficult project to completion.

A person cannot be satisfied with being fed, clothed, and maintained by the labor of others without making some suitable return to the society that supports him. Just because you do not find what suits you, to refuse to labor at all, is to act unworthy of yourself and your destiny.

PERSEVERENCE

When we see how much can be accomplished by the man or woman with only average ability who resolutely persists in the course of action toward fulfilling their life purpose, we can accurately assess the value of perseverance as a factor in success. How many individuals who have won renown in the world of literature, science, or art, many of whom the world calls geniuses, can claim with Sir Isaac Newton that they owe all their greatness and whatever they may have been able to accomplish to the virtue of perseverance? They were once as weak and helpless as any of us, once as destitute of wisdom and power as an infant. Their characters, which are now given to the world and will be to millions yet unborn as patterns of greatness and goodness, were made by that untiring perseverance which marked their whole lives. From childhood to age they knew no such word as fail.

Talent is desirable, but perseverance is more so. This should teach a great lesson of patience to those who are ready to sink in despair and have grown weary in their strivings for better things. There is a certain monotony in daily life, and there are those whose aims are high, but who lack the inward strength to stand true to them amid adversity. They are conquered by the routine, and disheartened by the discipline and labor that guard the prizes of life.

Men and women who have pursued the best of causes have had to fight their way to triumph through a long succession of failures. Often they have labored perseveringly without any glimpse of success in sight. The heroism they have displayed is to be measured, not so much by their successes, as by the opposition they have encountered and the courage with which they have maintained the struggle. Some of the great works of literature in which are stored away great masses of information are the results of persevering efforts, before which many minds would have cringed. Gibbon consumed nineteen years in writing his masterpiece (The History of the Decline and Fall of the Roman Empire). How many would have had the courage to persevere that length of time, even if they were certain of success at last? Courage, when combined with energy and perseverance, will overcome difficulties apparently insurmountable.

Go to the men and women of business, those of worth and influence, and ask them who shall have their confidence and support. They will tell you "the person who falters not by the wayside, who toils on in their calling against every barrier, whose eyes are `upward,' and whose motto is `excellence.'" But they shun those who are lazy, fearful and tentative. They would as soon trust the wind as such persons.

A common-sense author says, "Genius unexerted is no more genius than a bushel of acorns is a forest of oaks." There may be epics in men's brains, just as there are oaks in acorns, but the tree and the book must come out before we can measure them. Firmness of purpose is an indicator of a person's character and one of the best instruments of success. Without it, genius wastes its efforts in a maze of inconsistencies.

Some use circumstances as an excuse for failure while others force themselves on in spite of what is considered misfortune until circumstances become more favorable. A shrewd thinker has said, "Life is too short for us to waste one moment in deploring our lot." To become dejected in seasons of distress and difficulty is evidence of a weak mind. Opposing circumstances often create strength, both mental and physical. To overcome one barrier gives us greater ability to overcome the next. It is cowardice to grumble about circumstances.

It is wonderful to see what miracles a resolute and unyielding will can achieve. Before its irresistible force the most formidable obstacles become as cobweb barriers in the path. Difficulties that cause the irresolute to shrink back with dismay cause the person with determination to only smile. Those who start for glory must pursue their goal not only where there is a path, but also where there is none. And if they stumble, they should stumble forward.

One step after another will enable you to arrive at your journey's end, however long it may be. It is only when you count up the aggregate number of steps that you are ready to sink under a feeling of despair. But you are not required to take them all at once; there is an allotted time for each step. Always remember that the regular daily portions performed quietly and systematically, day after day, will enable you to achieve almost any desired result.

Regardless of your condition in life, you should aim high, and resolve to labor as necessary for its realization. You should cheerfully meet the trials and burdens that life has in store for you. When you learn to carry a thing through in all of its details, you have measured the secret of success. When you persevere, you force life to yield to you its grandest triumphs.

— ⚜ —

ENERGY

Energy is a force of character—an inward power. It introduces such a concentration of the will upon the realization of an idea that it crushes every opposing force that stands in the way of triumph. Energy knows of nothing but success. It will not listen to the voice of discouragement. Though it may perish beneath an avalanche of difficulties, it dies contending for its ideal.

The most common mistake a young person can make is to suppose that extraordinary talents are necessary to achieve more than ordinary success. If we are not careful, we may assume that the prizes of life are destined for only those with brilliant minds. However, people of seemingly mediocre power driven by the energy of purpose have often been able to accomplish extraordinary results. The people who have most powerfully influenced the world have been those with strong convictions, irresistible energy, invincible determination and an enduring capacity for work.

Energy that works toward accomplishment is what rules the world. There is more energy shown in quietly doing your duty through years of patient toil than to rush with great clamor at the obstacles of life, only to relinquish the attempt if success does not immediately crown the effort.

But such leaders are few, and for every one who seems to rule events, there are thousands who follow. Just as people in a crowd instinctively make room for one who seems to force his way through it, so mankind everywhere opens their ranks to one who pushes valiantly toward some object lying beyond them.

In order for energy to reach its highest development, it must be controlled by wisdom. Many discouraged people have expended sufficient energy for the highest success, but they have failed to reach their reward because they have not sought counsel at the lips of wisdom.

People of feeble action are accustomed to attributing their misfortune to what is termed *bad luck*. They envy the people who climb the ladder of prominence, and call them lucky. This is vain and foolish imagination. Energy produces good fortune and success, while laziness produces misfortune and bad luck.

You may have ambition enough to wish you were on the topmost step of the ladder of success, but if you don't have the energy to commence and push ahead, you will always remain on the lower steps of the ladder. There is a charm hidden in difficult undertakings that is appreciated only by those who dare to grapple with them.

Nothing can be more distasteful than to see people of apparently good abilities waiting for someone to come and help them over difficulties. If a rock rises up before you, roll it along or climb over it. If you want money, earn it. If you want confidence, prove yourself worthy of it. Don't be content with doing what has been done—surpass it. Deserve success and it will come.

If the job is long, the pay will be greater. If the task is hard, the more competent you must be to do it. Skillful pilots gain their reputation from storms. He who weakly shrinks from the struggle, who offers no resistance, who will not endure labor or fatigue, cannot fulfill his own potential or contribute to the general welfare of mankind.

66

It is folly for a man or woman to sit down in mid-life discouraged. True, it is a severe test of character to reflect that life has thus far proved a failure, but it does no good to despair. There are cobblestones in every road and pebbles in every path. It is energy that sheds the light of hope on the pathways and lightens life's load. All have cares, disappointments, and stumbling blocks. Crying, groaning, and regrets are of no avail. With energy and God's blessing it is possible to yet win a glorious victory. To make the most of life, it is necessary to make the aim high and noble and the energy tireless.

Would you make a success of life? Energy bids you to do with all your might what you have marked out as necessary to do and pursue it with resolution and vigor. Stick to the thing and carry it through. Believe you were made for the task, that no one else can do it, and you will succeed. You will think better of yourself, and others will think better of you.

⚜

ENTERPRISE

We are familiar with examples of men and women who have gained fortunes and renown because of some originality in their aims and methods. This enabled them to command the attention of a busy world long enough to gain from it the special object of their choice.

True enterprise is constantly on the alert to discover some new want of society, some fertile source of profit or honor, some unexplored field of business. It is nearly an indispensable element in these days of fierce competition. Every avenue of business is crowded, and as soon as it is known that someone has secured success by a particular method, there are scores of eager aspirants ready to try the successful plan. But, that too, ceases to be unique and becomes common, losing the power it formerly possessed of compelling success. Therefore, the latecomers in the field are doomed to failure even though they may be better fitted for the peculiar work at hand. What they should do is aim at success by new plans and methods.

Those who enlist to win life's battles must expect to wage the fight not only by the old methods but also by the new. To use only those tactics that are sanctioned by usage is to invite defeat. Throw open the windows of your mind to new ideas, and keep at least abreast of the times, and if possible, ahead of them. Nothing is more fatal to advancement than conservatism or imitation.

In business, you must know your trade and people. Spare no effort to master all the intricacies of the business or vocation in which you are engaged. Be alert to discover new ways to reach your desired goals. Whatever your calling, if you do not find markets you must make them. Every calling has bold men and women who are perpetually inventing new ways of attracting customers. The person who sticks doggedly to the old-fashioned methods—who runs in a perpetual rut—will find himself outstripped in the race of life.

Enterprise can be improved by cultivation, the same as physical strength or mental faculty. He who would excel as a swimmer must be often in the water. Do not hesitate to try plans simply because they are new, but be eager to put them to the test. If you find your life routine and commonplace, get to work devising some new way to change it.

It is enterprise that bids us to explore entirely new fields, discovering means that enable us to change what was fast becoming a failure into a glorious victory. In short, enterprise can lift the person with mediocre abilities and attainments into the foremost ranks of the successful ones.

⚜

PUNCTUALITY

This is a virtue that leads to success in life and yet some reckon it to be of little account. Success and happiness depend a lot more than most people suppose on punctuality. To be punctual in all of your appointments is a duty of common honesty. An appointment is a contract, and if you do not keep it you are dishonestly using other people's time and money. To a busy person, time is money. If you rob him of it, you have done him no less injury than if you had picked his pocket or paid him with a counterfeit bill.

Many people in business have been brought to bankruptcy and ruin by the failure of one person to meet his or her obligation promptly. To the person who meets his obligations promptly, whose word is as good as his bond, every avenue to success is open to him. No one can have a very high opinion of the person who has little regard for punctuality and leaves the impression that "it's no big deal." There are people who are otherwise worthy people, but who cannot command confidence because they are slack in fulfilling their engagements and meeting their obligations in small matters. They are daily losing ground among their peers because of this. A person will eventually be ruined this way.

Many of the most successful business people date their success from the time they commenced to practice this virtue. Thousands have failed in life from carelessness in this respect alone. Nothing inspires confidence in a person more than this quality; nor is there any habit that saps a reputation more than that of always being late. Punctuality is a virtue that can give force and power to an otherwise utterly insignificant character. Like charity, it covers a multitude of sins.

There is more to punctuality than just "being on time." A right estimate of the value of time is the best and surest foundation for habits of punctuality. Each hour as it passes swiftly away is gone *forever*. Lost wealth may be replaced by hard work. Lost friends may be regained by consideration and patience. Lost health may be recovered by medical skill and care. But lost time cannot be recovered.

If a person's time is properly occupied, every hour will have its appropriate activity or work. If the work of one hour is postponed to another, it must encroach upon the time for another duty or remain undone. Thus the whole day can be thrown into disorder. It is no wonder that the person who is habitually behind in the fulfillment of his duties

70

finds himself sinking under a load of accumulated cares. They eventually give up the battle and find themselves filling a subordinate place in the economy of the world.

When we put off or delay a certain work or duty, it usually leads to trouble. It is all too easy to put off today's work until tomorrow. But tomorrow has its own peculiar duties. The right thing must be done in the right way, but also at the right time, if we would reap the rewards of our labor.

The beginner in life should make this one of the first habits to acquire. If in youth it is not easy to be punctual, then later in life when the character is fixed, it is almost impossible to unlearn the habit of tardiness. The habit of punctuality, developed in youth and carried into life, is one of the main instruments for making your dreams come true.

≈⊙ ⚜ ⊙≈

CONCENTRATION

It is impossible to be successful in every branch of business, or renowned in every department of a profession. We must learn to focus our energies to one point, and to go directly to that point, looking neither to the right nor to the left. There are times when it is wise to leave things unknown and leave things undone. The person who would know one thing well must have the courage to be ignorant of a thousand other things, however attractive or interesting.

Take those names that are historic, and with the exception of a few great creative minds, you find them to be people who are identified with one achievement upon which their life force was spent. The great majority of men and women must concentrate their energies upon the complete mastery of one profession, trade, or calling, or they will experience the same disappointment as those whose empire has been lost in the ambition of universal conquest. In any trade or profession the most successful people have been those who have stuck to one thing. Those who are competent to do almost anything do nothing because they never make up their minds about what they want or who they intend to be. A person may have the most amazing talents, but if they are scattered upon many objects he will accomplish nothing. It is an indisputable fact that more people fail from a multiplicity of pursuits than from a poverty of resources.

Engage in one kind of business only, and stick to it until you succeed, or until your experience shows that you should abandon it. When a person's undivided attention is centered on one object, his mind will be constantly suggesting improvements of value that would escape him were his brain occupied by a dozen different objects at once. There is good sense in the old caution against having too many irons in the fire at once. To be effective, concentrated aim is needed. The marksman who aims at the whole target will seldom hit its center.

The gardener does not allow the sap to be driven into a thousand channels merely to develop a bunch of profitless twigs. He prunes the branches, allowing the vital juices to be absorbed by a few vigorous fruit-bearing branches.

The author or philosopher may revel among the sweetest and most beautiful flowers of thought, but unless he gathers and condenses them into the honeycomb of some great thought or work, his finest conceptions will be lost and useless.

The time spent by many people in profitless reading would, if concentrated on a single line of study, have made them masters of an entire branch of literature or science.

Concentration is a great safeguard against exhaustion. He who scatters himself on many objects soon loses his energy, and with his energy, his enthusiasm, and how is success possible without enthusiasm? Therefore, cultivate the habit of concentration so that it becomes second nature.

***

DECISION

There are those who seem to precede the march of events and have the foresight to seize the moment for action that others use in deliberation. There are occasions when action must be taken at once. There is no time for long and careful calculation of chances. While hesitating and deliberating, the occasion goes by, in most cases never to return again. At such times is seen the triumph of those who will seize the occasion to execute a plan of action.

There are times when caution and delay are necessary, when to act without long and careful deliberation would be madness. But when the way is clear and there is no doubt as to what ought to be done, we must decide promptly and move ahead.

To do anything in this world that is worth doing we must not stand shivering on the bank, thinking of the cold and danger, but jump in and scramble through as best we can. Every person will encounter obstacles and difficulties that must be conquered. Hesitation is a sign of weakness and it is better to occasionally decide wrongly than to be forever wavering and hesitating, veering to this side or that, with all the misery and disaster that follow from continual doubt.

It is scarcely possible to conceive of a more unhappy person than one who is always brooding over his plans, but never executing them—who is always intending to lead a new life, but never finds the time to set about it. Many are the valiant purposes that end merely in words; deeds intended that are never done; projects that are never begun, and all for the lack of a little courageous decision. The most decisive answer of all is *doing*.

We admire the person who makes up his mind and sticks to it, who sees what needs to be done and does it. The vacillating person, no matter what his or her abilities, is invariably pushed aside in the race of life by one with a determined will. It is the person who resolves to succeed, and at every fresh rebuff begins resolutely again, that reaches the goal. There have been people with brilliant abilities who lacked courage, faith, and decision that failed while

74

more resolute, but less capable adventurers, succeeded. Many people go to their graves in obscurity only because they lacked the resolve to begin, to make the first effort, and would have astonished the world by their achievements and successes.

THE ABILITY TO THINK

The thoughtless and impulsive acts of today result in a tomorrow full of regrets. Young people often exhibit a natural impulsiveness that can be highly detrimental to their best interests. Personal usefulness depends upon our impulses being controlled and subject to good judgment.

The ability to carefully consider every desire and impulse that rises from within before acting upon it is an element of safety found nowhere else. Many lives are wrecked through thoughtlessness alone. Think before you act. At every action, ask yourself, "What will be the consequences of this? Am I likely to regret it?" Whatever you do, remember the end, and you will never go amiss.

Young people who are taught *how* to think will soon learn *what* to think. A person who cannot command his thoughts shouldn't expect to control his actions. All mental superiority originates in habits of thought. It is of great importance that right habits of thought be formed and nurtured early in life. Think of things pure and lovely and of good report; think of

God and of heaven, and your life will be full of good deeds and pleasant memories.

～◎ ⚜ ◎～

A TRAINED MIND

The lack of mental training and discipline explains why we so often meet people who are the possessors of vast stores of knowledge, and yet fail at everything they try. The most learned person does not always make the best teacher. The lawyer who has received the best classical education is not always the most successful. The people who have been in power have not always been graduates.

Education accomplishes wonders in fitting a person for the work of success, but we sometimes forget that it is better to have the mind well disciplined than richly stored. It is not uncommon to see a person of high culture outdistanced in the race of life by an upstart who cannot spell. Men and women have ruled well who could not define a commonwealth, and they who did not understand the shape of the earth have commanded a greater portion of it.

A person with knowledge who has failed to practically apply the knowledge is no better off than the person who doesn't possess the knowledge. It is not the amount of knowledge, but the capacity to *apply* it, which promises success and usefulness in life. Knowledge merely gathered together, whether in books or in brains, is devoid of power unless

76

quickened to life by the thoughts and actions of some practical worker.

Intellectual knowledge is to be prized, but practical training is necessary to make it available. Brilliance has often existed in those lacking what may be called common sense. The old sailor knows nothing of nautical astronomy. But he can scan the seas and skies and warn of coming danger with a natural wisdom, which all the keen intellect and ready mathematics of the young lieutenant do not afford.

The person in his study with his pen in hand may show himself capable of forming large views of life and policy, but may in the outer world be found altogether unfitted for putting them into practice. The mere theorist rarely displays practical ability and the practical person rarely displays a high degree of theoretical wisdom.

Practical people cut the knots they can't untie.

Unless education is practical, it fails to prepare a person for contest with others. Practical wisdom is learned in the school of experience. Precepts and instruction are useful as far as they go, but without the discipline of real life experience they remain theories only. Practical knowledge will not always by itself raise a person to eminence, but for lack of it many have fallen short of distinction.

Education must be regarded as a means and not as an end. By education *and* experience we can convert that which lay dormant as a rough pebble into a dazzling diamond. Practical talents are a gift of God, and we can cultivate them to perfection.

People are often like knives with many blades. They know how to open one and only one blade. The rest are buried in the handle and become useless. Practical education is the knowledge of how to use each blade—how to open it, keep it sharp, and apply it to all practical purposes.

Education is not simply instruction, facts, and rules communicated by a teacher. A good education wakes up and develops latent powers resulting in a growth of the mind. It finds the mind passive and trains it to think independently. It awakens the power to observe, to reflect, and to combine.

By gaining an education you have as your reward rich stores of knowledge that will always be at your command and more valuable than material treasures. While riches may fade, the intellectual stores you have gathered will be permanent and enduring—a bank whose dividends are perpetual, whose wealth is undiminished no matter how frequent the drafts made upon it. How wise is it then to secure a complete and lasting education.

Too many have swallowed the idea that an education may be obtained only within the walls of some classical school and that their careers must be commenced with a college diploma. Our education is by no means entirely the product of organized schools, hired teachers and printed books. When considering how a person's learning prepared him for practical success, it is often discovered that the most useful items weren't covered in the education that his father paid for.

While we ought to remember that there is a discipline afforded by books and study, there is also a life education—that great common arena where men and women do battle with the forces around them everyday. Life is one grand school, and every circumstance is a teacher. Every day gives us many lessons in life. Some are educated in vice, some in folly, some in selfishness, some in deception, some in goodness and truth.

We are influenced by society and it is our duty to guide and control these influences so that we are educated in the right direction. If we are lax in this duty to ourselves and let the world educate us as it will, we are running the risk of yielding to the circumstances life throws at us and allowing ourselves to drift with the current.

Therefore, we cannot be too careful to have our education proceed in the right direction. Error is more hopeless than ignorance. Ignorance is a blank sheet on which we can write, but error is a scribbled one from which we must first erase. Ignorance is content to stand still without advancing towards wisdom, but error being more presumptuous, proceeds in a wrong direction and then must retrace her steps. Consequently, she has a longer way to go than ignorance in the acquisition of truth.

Education should involve the whole person—the body, the mind, and the heart. A well-developed tree is not one simply well rooted, or with giant branches, or rich foliage, but all three of these together.

Guard your health because a feeble body acts powerfully on the mind and is a hindrance to its progress. The body is just as important a factor as the mind in the work of success and just as worthy to be improved. You might as well try to enjoy life in a run-down house that allows free admission to the freezing blast and pouring rain as to be happy in a body ruined by self-indulgence. If God has given you good health and a sound mind, it is your duty to do all you can to preserve it so that it will perform all the necessary functions in the great work of life.

It is common in this age to educate the head, and forget the more important education of the heart. Is the *head* more important than the *heart*? While it may be true that wealth is the child of one, it is also true that happiness is the child of the other.

Education is within the reach of all. The young person that believes it is impossible for him to get an education is deficient in courage and energy. There is no excuse for a youth to grow up to adulthood and its duties with an untrained mind having not received the advantages of a practical education.

Some may think they are excused by poverty, but a lack of means doesn't deprive them of a single intellectual power. On the contrary, it sharpens them. Has poverty shut them out from nature, from truth, from God? One can live a lifetime and get no instruction, but as soon as he begins to look for wisdom, it is given him. One flower opens its cup and takes in the dew while another closes itself and the drop runs off. God rains his wisdom as widespread as the dew, and if we lack wisdom, it is because we refuse to open our hearts and receive it.

Ignorance is a voluntary misfortune, for all who want to may drink deeply at the fountain of knowledge. Whoever is determined to cultivate his mind will not find anything sufficient to stop him. A person who does not form the habit of reading, observation, and reflection will go through this life none the wiser for all the wonders that are around him.

In our libraries we meet great minds and feel at ease with them. We come to know them better, perhaps, than those who bear their names and share their home. No carelessness of manner, no poverty of speech or unfortunate personal peculiarity, mars the relationship of author and reader. It is a relationship in which the exchange of thought is undisturbed by outward conditions. We lose our narrow selves in a broader life that is opened to us.

Books are a guide to youth and an inspiration for age. They support us in solitude, and keep us from becoming a burden to ourselves. They lessen our cares and lay our disappointments to rest.

The best writers give their readers the most knowledge and take from them the least amount of time. The books which are the most profitable to read are those which make the reader think the most.

While most great minds have been very devout readers, reading is not profitable without meditation. By reading you gather food for thoughts, principles, and actions. If our books are wisely selected and properly studied, they will enlighten our minds, improve our hearts, and establish our characters. Each of us should be like the person who works in the diamond mine, who casts away all that is worthless, keeping only the pure and precious gems.

Although the following concentrates on books and what we read, today this can be expanded to include what we listen to and watch e.g. radio, podcasts, television and videos, etc.

The world is full of books, many of which are either worthless or hurtful. Good books are as scarce as good companions. We should choose our books as we do our friends. Some books we should make our constant companions taking them with us wherever we go by keeping them in our hands or in our hearts. Others we should receive only as occasional acquaintances and visitors. Some are full of depravity and we should shun them as we would the actual vices that they represent.

You may judge a person more truly by what he reads, listens to, and watches than by the company he keeps—for his associates are in some measure imposed upon him, but his reading and entertainment is usually the result of choice. We should all realize that that we are unconsciously influenced by their opinions and trained to their way of thinking.

Nobody can too highly appreciate the power of the press or media. Nor can they too highly depreciate their abuse of power. They exert a controlling influence over a nation, catering the everyday food of the mind that impresses an indelible mark upon the lives and conduct of its citizens.

A person may see, hear, or read whatever he pleases, but he will know very little beyond that which he has thought over and made the property of his own mind. We should treasure most those moments that are employed in developing our own thoughts, rather than in acquiring those of others. Knowledge acquired by labor becomes a possession —a property entirely our own. But if to avoid the trouble of a search we avail ourselves of the superior information of someone else, such knowledge will not likely remain with us for we have *borrowed* it and not *bought* it.

You may strengthen your intellect by reading, reflection, and writing down your thoughts. One book read thoroughly and with careful reflection will do more to improve the mind and enrich the understanding than skimming over the surface of a whole library. You may glean knowledge by reading, but you must separate the chaff from the wheat by thinking. The more one reads in a busy, superficial manner, the worse. It is like loading the stomach with a great quantity of food, which lies there, undigested. Undigested knowledge is as oppressive as undigested food. Thought is to the brain what gastric juice is to the stomach—an enzyme to reduce whatever is received to a condition in which all that is wholesome and nutritious may be appropriated. It is not what a person eats, but what he digests that makes him strong; not what he earns, but what he saves that makes him rich; so it is not what he reads or hears, but what he remembers *and* applies that makes him wise. The fruit of meditation is appropriate action.

When you read, make careful observations and select subjects upon which your thoughts may dwell when you have laid the book aside. He who reads only for present gratification, and neglects to digest what he reads, nor calls it up for future contemplation, will not likely ever know the extent of his own powers because the best method to make them known will remain unemployed. It is in this kind of intellectual exercise that our powers are best brought into action and disciplined for use. Become master of your thoughts so that you can command them at your pleasure.

The mind must be trained to think and remember. Memory is a valuable and mysterious gift that God has given us, and it may be improved by anyone who will take the necessary steps. The more it is exercised, the more it is able to do. There seems to be no limit to its power. Memory must be ready with her stores of knowledge. She must be trained to classify and arrange facts so that they may be recalled and examined with ease when wanted.

If the mind is not cultivated into a beautiful garden, it will become overrun with weeds and wild flowers. We must guard against indulging in thoughts that would stain our character if they become settled habits. It has been wisely ordained that light should have no color, water no taste, air no odor and knowledge should be equally pure. Impure thoughts are seeds of sin. If dropped into the soil of the mind, they will germinate, spring up, and bear the fruits of sinful words and acts. Few consider the power and magnitude of thought.

Man is as he thinks. Deeds make a reputation; thoughts make a character. Thoughts surpass deeds in power and grandeur in the same ratio as character surpasses reputation.

We sometimes hang back because it takes so long to acquire a mastery of anything. Let the end alone! Begin at the beginning and even if after all is done, you are informed on only one point more, your life will be happier for having made the effort.

WISE CHOICE OF COMPANIONS

The chameleon changes its color to agree with that of surrounding objects. All of us by nature possess this quality to such a degree that our character, habits, and principles take their form and color from those of our intimate associates. Association with people wiser, better, and more experienced than ourselves is always inspiring and invigorating. They enhance our knowledge of life. We become partners in their wisdom and enlarge our field of observation through their eyes. We profit by their experiences and are instructed by what they have suffered. Hence companionship with the wise has a valuable influence on the foundation of character.

The company you keep is both an indicator and former of your character. Young people are little aware how much their reputation is affected by the company they keep. The character of their associates is soon regarded as their own. Seek to be the companion of those who fear God. Then you will be wise.

It is better to be alone than in bad company. The mind is just as susceptible to infections as the body. Bad company is like a nail driven into a post, which, after the first or second blow, may be drawn out with little difficulty. But if it is driven all the way in to the head, it can only be withdrawn by the destruction of the wood. Evil company is like tobacco smoke. You cannot be long in its presence without carrying away a smell of it.

It is not only the vulgar and profane whose example and association pose a danger. There are persons of apparently decent morals, polished manners, and interesting talents who are unprincipled. They make light of sacred things and scoff at religion. They rejoice to see youthful virtue and parental hope wither and die. These are the persons whose association and influence are to be feared the most.

※ ✚ ☙

FRIENDSHIP

Friendship improves happiness and relieves misery by doubling our joys and dividing our griefs. Friendship produces a mutual inclination between two or more persons to promote each other's interests, knowledge, virtue, and happiness.

The language of friendship is as varied as the wants and weaknesses of humanity. To the timid and cautious it speaks words of encouragement. To the weak it is ready to extend a helping hand. To the bold and venturesome it whispers words of caution. It is ready to sympathize with the sorrowing one, and to rejoice with those of good cheer.

The first law of friendship is sincerity, and he who violates this law will soon find himself destitute of that which he sought. If you would win friends, be steady and true to yourself. Be the unfailing friend of your own purposes, stand by your own character, and others will come to your aid. Who is not a friend to the person who is a friend to himself or herself?

Few persons are fortunate enough to secure in the course of life even one devoted and true friend. One true friend is worth a whole caravan of those lukewarm souls, who although they profess to be a friend, their affection is so uncertain that we fear putting it to the test and risk losing it forever.

Prosperity is no just scale; adversity is the only true balance to weigh friends in. True friendship must withstand the shocks of adversity before it is entitled to the name. Friendships born in adversity are more firm and lasting than those formed in happiness, just as iron is more strongly united the fiercer the flames. Real friends visit us in prosperity only when invited, but in adversity they come of their own accord. If we lack the wisdom to discriminate between our acquaintances and our friends, misfortune will do it for us. Prosperity gains friends while adversity tests them. False friends are like our shadows—keeping close to us while we walk in the sunshine, but disappearing the instant we cross into the shade.

It is hard for those who fall from affluence to poverty and obscurity to discover that the attachment of so many in whom they confided was a pretense, a mask to gain their own ends. Flies leave the kitchen when the dishes are empty. The parasites that cluster around the favorites of fortune linger with the sunshine, but scatter at the approach of a storm, just as the leaves cling to a tree in the summer, but drop off at the breath of winter.

Consider the one you call your friend: will he weep with you in your hours of distress? Will he faithfully reprove you to your face for actions that others are ridiculing and condemning you behind your back? Will he dare stand up in your defense when detractors are secretly aiming their weapons at your reputation? If you should suffer financial loss, will he still be happy in your company or withdraw himself now from such an unprofitable relationship? Will he still take pleasure in professing to be your friend, and cheerfully assist you to support the burden of your afflictions? When sickness visits you, will he listen with attention to your tale of suffering, and administer comfort and consolation to your fainting spirit? And lastly, when death shall burst asunder every earthly tie, will he shed a tear upon your grave, and lodge the dear remembrance of your friendship in his heart? If so, then you know the privilege of having one true friend.

It is more difficult to find a devoted friend when we need one. Cling to your friends after having chosen them with proper caution. If they reprove you, thank them; if they grieve you, forgive them; if circumstances have torn them from you, circumstances may change and make them yours again. Be very slow to give up an old, tried and trusted friend. A true friend is such a rare thing to have that you are blessed beyond measure if you possess just one.

GOOD HABITS

Habit is a person's best friend or worst enemy. It can exalt you to the highest pinnacle of virtue, honor, and happiness, or sink you to the lowest depths of vice, shame, and misery.

Habits influence us more by their frequent recurrences than by their importance.

Those people who develop a habit by constant repetition of an action appear to have lost their free will.

As we get older, habits govern without control and they cannot be contradicted without uneasiness.

There are many who find themselves slaves to a bad habit who would gladly give money and time to be free from its control.

Always remember that a bad habit, when opposed, offers the most vigorous resistance on the first attack. At each successive encounter this resistance grows weaker until, finally, it ceases altogether, and victory is achieved.

The power of a new habit is such that it renders pleasant something that at first was intensely disagreeable or even painful.

Happiness can even become a habit. One may acquire the habit of looking upon the bright side of things or looking on the gloomy side.

Recognizing the power of habits, it should be plain to all the importance of forming habits that will increase our happiness and make certain our success in the endeavors of life. Habits that are to be commended are not formed in a day, but by steady, persistent efforts. Above all, they should be acquired in youth, for then they cost the least effort. Like letters cut in the bark of a tree, they grow and widen with age.

⚜

PERSONAL INFLUENCE

"I shot an arrow in the air;
It fell on earth, I knew not where.

I breathed a song into the air;
It fell on earth, I knew not where.

Long, long afterwards, in an oak,
I found the arrow still unbroke.

And the song, from beginning to end,

I found again in the heart of a friend.
---H. W. Longfellow

Just as the blossom doesn't know what becomes of the fragrance that is carried away by the wind, a person doesn't know the limit of influence which constantly and imperceptibly escapes from his daily life going far beyond his conscious thoughts. Influence is to a person what flavor is to fruit, or fragrance is to the flower. It does not develop or determine character, but it is the measure of a person's interior richness and worth. Influence is a power we exert over others by our thoughts, words, and actions; in short, by our lives. Some men fill the air with their presence and sweetness, as orchards in October fill the air with the perfume of ripe fruits. Some women fill their homes with the fragrance of their goodness like honeysuckle sweetens the entire place. Such men and women are trees of righteousness, which are ever dropping precious fruit all around them.

Your influence is not confined to the scene of your immediate actions; it extends to others, and will reach to succeeding ages. Future generations will feel the influence of your conduct. The best inheritance a parent can leave a child is a virtuous example. Let parents always remember this.

Everything leaves a history and an influence. The rolling rock leaves its scratches on the mountain, the river its channel in the soil, the animal its bones in the stratum. We live and we die, but the good or evil we do lives on after us.

The golden words that good men and women have spoken, and the examples they have set, live through all time. They pass into the thoughts and hearts of their successors, helping them on the road of life. They call us to walk in the paths that they have trod—to guide, influence and direct us.

A person's friends, family, and successors in office are all receptive of a moral influence—either a blessing that will repeat itself in showers of blessing, or a curse that will multiply itself in ever-accumulating evil.

You cannot move people until you are one of them. They will not follow you until they have heard your voice, shaken your hand, and fully learned your principles and your sympathies. It makes no difference how much you know or how much you are capable of doing. You may pile accomplishments a mile high, but if you fail to be a social person, demonstrating that your lot is with the rest of society, then a little child with a song or a kiss for all and a pair of innocent hands to lay upon the knee shall lead more hearts and change the direction of more lives than you.

Shall your influence be for good? Then let no act of yours lead another person astray. It is a terrible thought that some careless word, even uttered in jest, might start some soul upon the downward road. We cannot live to ourselves. We must always remember that there is one record we cannot change —our lives written on others' hearts. How gladly we would review and write a kind word here, a generous act there, erase a frown and put in a loving word, a bright smile, or a tender expression.

Harshness would be erased, and gentleness written. But sadly, what is written is written.

⚜

A GOOD CHARACTER

A good character is a precious thing, above rubies, gold, crowns, or kingdoms. A good name is to be chosen rather than great riches. It is better to be poor than to be destitute of a good name, and endure the pains of a conscious worthlessness of character.

A good name is the richest possession you have while living, and the best inheritance you leave behind when you are gone.

While a good name may be inherited from parents, it must be upheld by ones own endeavors. A good character is in all cases the fruit of personal exertion and not an appendage of birth, wealth, talents, or station in life. Nothing can be more fatal to the attainment of a good name than confidence in external advantages. Rather it is the fruit and reward of a life of goodness manifested by virtuous and honorable actions. Therefore, the attainment of a good name is within the reach of all.

A good name, which has cost many years to establish, is often destroyed in a single hour. A good name is gained by many actions, but lost by one.

The mind is the blank page; character is the writing we put on it. The mind is the shop; character is the profits of the trade.

Whether a character is good or bad, it has been long in the making. By repetition of acts, the character becomes slowly but decidedly formed. Even the secret thought never expressed, the inward indulgence in imaginary wrong, the lie never told for lack of courage, the immorality never indulged in for fear of public rebuke are just as effectual in staining the heart as though the world knew all about them. Though you may never give them outward expression, if you harbor in your heart all manners of evil thoughts, they will be potent in shaping your character. Society at large may be less injured by the latent existence of evil than by its public expression, but the individual is as much injured by cherished thoughts of evil as by the open commission of it, and sometimes even more.

One of the most essential elements of a good name is the possession of good moral principles. A character without fixed moral principles is defective. Lacking such principles one would seek in vain to acquire a good name. Such a person is like a ship crossing the ocean to a destined harbor with no rudder to control its course.

Our principles are the source of our actions and our actions are the source of our happiness or misery. We cannot, therefore, be too careful in establishing our principles. Men and women of integrity and high principles command the respect of everyone. It is natural to have confidence in them and to imitate them. Virtuous principles are the basis of a good moral character and the person who possesses such character can be trusted.

A person with a principled character displays independence. He or she thinks and acts as an individual and is not made to serve the purpose of the group. A principled person is diligent in doing what he knows is right. What he is today he will be tomorrow. But the unprincipled person is often perplexed in deciding on a plan of action. Questions regarding personal interests or popularity thicken around him.

Principles do not change with the times or circumstances. They are the same yesterday, today and forever. They may be applied by people of all walks of life, the learned and the ignorant, the beggar and the rich.

A person who is ruled by principles secures self-respect. He is not degraded in his own eyes by acting from unworthy and criminal motives. It is only when self-respect is lost that you fully comprehend its value. It is the fruit of doing what is right.

The love of money exerts a powerful influence over people. When money is the governing principle of conduct, it is not expected that a person will be very honorable in the means of obtaining it. Hold a piece of gold too close to the eye and it is large enough to blind you to home, to love, to death, and to heaven itself.

The principles adopted when we are young become second nature, shaping the course of our life and exerting a decisive influence on whether we succeed or fail. A young person who is loose in his principles and habits, who lives without a plan or goals, and spends his time in idleness and pleasure is sure to become a worthless character.

To have a character based on good principles is the first and indispensable qualification of a good citizen. If a young person passes the critical period of life, from ages fourteen to twenty-one, with pure morals and an untarnished reputation, a good name is almost sure to crown his years and follow him the rest of his days.

The individual, the community, and the nation, show their true worth, in the eyes of God, by their estimation of character. Whenever character is made a secondary concern, sensualism and crime prevail. Anyone who enters upon any study, pursuit, amusement, pleasure, habit, or course of life, without considering its effect upon his character is not a trustworthy or an honest person. As a person prizes his character, so is he.

There is a difference between character and reputation. Character is what a person is; reputation is what he is thought to be. Character is within; reputation is without. Character is always real; reputation may be false. Character is substantial and enduring; reputation may be vapory and fleeting. Character is at home; reputation is abroad. Character is in a person's own soul; reputation is in the minds of others. Character is the solid food of life; reputation is the dessert. Character is what gives a person value in his own eyes; reputation is what he is valued at in the eyes of others. Character is his real worth; reputation is his market price.

A person may have a good character and a bad reputation; or he may have a good reputation and a bad character because we form our opinion of people from what they appear to be, and not from what they really are. A person of good character is generally a person of good reputation, but this is not always the case. The motives and actions of the best person are sometimes misunderstood and misrepresented. It is important that we be right and do right, whether our motives and actions are properly understood and appreciated or not. Most people are more anxious about their reputation than they are about their character. This is not right. Nothing should be as important to a person as the formation and possession of a good character.

A person of good character is a person of honor. He whose soul is set to do right finds himself more firmly bound by the principle of honor than by legal restraints. His word is as good as his bond. Even if there is no law in the land one might deal just as safely with him. To take unfair advantage is not in him. His speeches are never riddles. He looks you in the eye and says straight out the things he has to say. He does unto others the things he would have them do to him. He is a good son and a good brother. With his friends, he proves himself true and does not betray their trust. You do not find him too curious about the affairs of others, or too eager to impart information gathered accidentally.

A good character is a sure protection against suspicion and evil reports. A person of bad or doubtful character is suspected of a thousand acts of which he may not be guilty. And if he does a good deed he is suspected of having a bad motive. He has lost the confidence of others. They know him to be unprincipled and hollow-hearted, and are therefore ready to believe all the evil that is thought or said of him, but none of the good.

On the other hand, a person of good character, with a tried and established reputation, stands out in the eyes of the public as one who is above suspicion and reproach. The envious may attempt to tarnish his good name, but their efforts recoil upon their own heads. Slander may, for a moment, fix its fangs on a spotless character, but such a character has within itself an antidote to the poison, and emerges from the temporary shadow with invigorated strength.

The principle of double-dealing is characteristic of this age. Its leading maxim is, "The end justifies the means" and, in pursuing its end, stops at nothing that promises success. One thing is said, and another thing is meant. With flattering lips and a double heart they speak. Their language and conduct do not proceed from fixed principles, but from a spirit of duplicity and selfishness. Nothing can be more fatal to character and success in life than to acquire the reputation as an artful dodger, one who does all things with an ulterior motive to further his own ends. He may succeed for a time, but he will soon be found out, and when found out will be despised.

A good name will also extend your sphere of usefulness. Books are useful only when they are read; sermons are influential only when they are listened to; but the weight of a person's character is felt by every one who comes within its sphere. Character is power and influence, and the person who has character has a means to be eminently useful to his friends and to society.

Who are the persons whose friendship is most highly valued, whose opinions carry the greatest weight, whose patronage is most eagerly sought, and whose influence is most desired? A good name draws around its possessor warm friends, and opens for him a sure path to wealth, honor, and happiness.

There are trying and perilous circumstances in life which show how valuable and important a good character is. It is a strong and sure staff of support when everything else fails. In the crisis of temptation, in the battle of life, when the struggle comes either from within or without, it is the strength of our character that defends and secures our happiness and honor.

A good character is the grandest thing a person can live for. The person who strives for greatness of character will not fail to receive a reward. This lesson is the first that youth should learn and the last that age should forget.

⚜

TRUE GREATNESS

So much in the world is artificial and glitters in borrowed light so that it is hard to discern between the true and the false. True greatness displays itself in good deeds. Matthew Henry said, "Nothing can make a man truly great but being truly good, and partaking of God's holiness." The greatest man or woman is the one who chooses right with an unshakable conviction.

Some people, however, are great only in their ability to do evil. Such appears to have constituted the greatness of many of those individuals who drenched the world in blood that their ambition might be satisfied. A person of the most brilliant qualities needs only a mixture of pride, ambition, and selfishness to be great in evil ways.

A truly great person is just and upright in his business dealings, in his public actions, and in his family life. He will be honest in all things—in his works and in his words. He will be generous and merciful to his opponent—to those who are weaker as well as those stronger than him.

True greatness is always modest in expression. The grace of an action is gone as soon as we are convinced it was done only that others might applaud the act. But he who is truly great does good because it is his duty and not so that others will witness his acts. His aim is to do good because it is right. There is more true greatness in duty faithfully done than in any one great act when others are looking on and giving their approval. The greatest people are often little known. The veil of oblivion successfully hides the greater portion of their lives.

A truly great person has a spirit of kindness. He is generous and tenderhearted. He seeks to relieve the misery of others as he would his own. Kindness is the most powerful instrument in the world to move a person's heart, and speaking a word of kindness will often do more for the furtherance of your cause than any amount of angry reasoning. The person whose whole life is spent in the exercise of kindness possesses a peculiar power and influence over the lives of others that marks them as one of the truly great.

FRUGALITY

Frugality may be termed the daughter of Prudence, the sister of Temperance, and the parent of Liberty and Ease. To the poor she is indispensable; to those of moderate means she is representative of wisdom.

Frugality is her best when joined to liberality. The first leaves off excessive expense; the last bestows them to the benefit of those in need. The first without the last leads to covetousness; the last without the first leads to extravagance.

By frugality the loaf is multiplied. Little becomes much, and out of next to nothing comes the miracle of something. Frugality is not merely saving. It is foresight and insight. It is a philosophy by which new uses are discovered. It causes useless things to serve our necessities, perishing things to renew their vigor, and all things to exert themselves for human comfort.

As the acquisition of knowledge depends more upon what a man *remembers* than upon the quantity of his reading, so the acquisition of property depends more upon what is *saved* than upon what is earned. The largest reservoir, though fed by abundant and living springs, will fail to supply their owners with water if secret leaking-places are permitted to drain off their contents. In like manner, even though a skilled and energetic person may have a very large source of income, through numerous wants and wasteful habits, he may live and die poor. Frugality is the guardian of property, the genius that guides the footsteps of every prosperous and successful person.

Frugality is especially commendable in the person who struggles with poverty, and must be practiced if he desires to secure independence and happiness. Simple work and thrift will go a long way towards making any person of ordinary working faculties comparatively independent in his means.

It is not meant that a person deny himself every amusement, every recreation, or every comfort, but he must be willing to deny himself some luxuries and save to lay a base of independence in the future. If a person defies the future, and spends all that he earns, whether much or little, let him look for lean and hungry times in the future, for they will surely come, no matter what he thinks.

Frugality foresees emergencies and provides against them. To spend all that you acquire as soon as you gain it is to lead a butterfly existence. If you were always young and free from sickness and care, and life were to pass as one perpetual Summer, it would do no harm to so live; but you know life has its Autumn and Winter as well as its Summer. Some people are bound to learn in their latter years the lessons of strict economy for the first time, having lived in utter defiance of them in the season of youth and strength.

If you fail to live within your income, poverty will accompany you through life. We urge all young people who are just starting in life to make it an invariable rule to lay aside a certain portion of their income, whatever that income may be. Expenditures, no matter how small they may be, are always extravagant when they come fully up to the entire amount of a person's income. The great secret of being prosperous and comfortable is to get ahead of your expenses.

Eat and drink this month what you earned last month, not what you are going to earn next month. It is unsafe to draw drafts on the future.

When one is weighed down with a load of debt, he loses the sense of being free and independent. A person who has a fine house, a new car and many parties, for which he is in debt, is a slave dragging chains behind him through all the grandeur of the fake world through which he moves.

Those who strive by outward appearances to carry an impression of wealth and position beyond their real income are compelled by their lavish expenditures to a strict economy in seclusion. If they were to exercise strict economy at all times, they would soon be placed in that position they so much long for.

A sober survey of one's expenditures as compared with his income; a wise balancing of goals to be attained; a determination to break habits that are opposed to good sense; and a patience that tolerates small and gradual results, will do much towards establishing the principle of economy and securing its benefits.

PATIENCE

Patience is the stabilizer of the soul that will keep it from rolling and tumbling in the greatest storms. Troubles and sorrows are in store for all. It is well that we don't try to escape them, as they seem essential to the perfection and development of a good character.

Patience is a quality graciously inherent in the heart of a person, *or* it must be acquired by the lessons of experience. Of all the lessons that life teaches us, the hardest is to wait.

There is no road too long for the person who advances deliberately and without undue haste. He that has patience can have what he desires. There are no honors too distant for the person who prepares for them with patience.

The history of all who are honored in the world of literature, arts, or science is the history of patient study for years, and its final triumph. Courage would have turned into despair and the world would have remained unimproved if the effect of a single stroke of the chisel had been compared with the pyramid to be raised, or a single impression of the spade compared with the mountain to be leveled. If we continuously apply ourselves, we cannot fail to steadily advance, though it may be unconsciously.

A sailboat cannot circumnavigate the world by one wind. The grandest results cannot be achieved in a day. The fruit that is the sweetest usually ripens the slowest. Therefore, everyone who wants to be successful must learn "to labor and to wait."

Let patience have her perfect work in the home circle. Let parents be patient with their children. They are weak and you are strong. They stand at the eastern gate of life and experience has not taught them to speak carefully and walk softly. What if their play and amusement grates upon your nerves? Bear with them patiently. Care and time will soon enough check their childish impulses.

Be patient with your friends. They are not omniscient and cannot see your heart and may misunderstand you. They do not know what is best for you, and may select what is worst.

Above all, be patient with your beloved. Love is the best thing on earth; but it is to be handled tenderly, and impatience kills it. Try to smooth life's weary way for each other, and in the exercise of the heaven-born virtue of patience you will find the sweetest pleasures of life.

Impatience accomplishes nothing that is of value. It divides our efforts, frustrates our plans, and generally succeeds in making not only our lives miserable, but also all those around us.

Patience enables us to lessen the pains of mind and body. These things are killed by enduring them, but made strong to bite and sting by feeding them with your fears. There is no pain or care that can last long. None of them shall enter the city of God. In a little while you shall leave behind all your troubles, and forget that such things were on earth.

⚜

SELF-CONTROL

Self-control is the application of reason to all the daily acts of life. By abstaining from *most* things it is surprising how many things we can still enjoy.

Self-control is the physician of the soul as well as the body; and the universal medicine of life. It leads to and maintains health. This is a law that every youth should know *and* remember.

A lack of self-control is the fruitful mother of 90% of the diseases that our bodies suffer and the sins that we commit. All excesses grow from a lack of self-control. Bodily pains and aches tell of excess in some direction. Penalty follows excess and means that its sufferer should reform. The law of temperance cannot be broken with impunity. The excess may be committed today, but the effect is experienced tomorrow. The punishment is mild at first, but afterwards more and more severe, until, when nature's warning voice has been unheeded

106

and her punishments disregarded, the final penalty is death. If a billboard were hung out for the benefit of the young, there would be inscribed on it in prominent letters "NO EXCESS."

It must be remembered that the best principles, if pushed too far degenerate into fatal vices. Generosity is closely allied to extravagance; charity itself may lead to ruin; the sternness of discipline is but one step removed from oppression.

The person who wants self-control as a virtue must master himself. No person is free who doesn't have command over himself, but allows his appetites or his temper to control him. He must also remember that the field of temperance is a broad one, covering the whole area of life. It is not simply against one form of appetite, but he must guard against all indulgences. To triumph over these is the most glorious of all conquests. If a man or woman reigns within, and rules passions, desires, and fears, he is more than a king; she is more than a queen.

True wisdom seeks to restrain one from blindly following his impulses and appetites. To be morally free—to be more than an animal—a person must be able to resist instinctive impulses. This can only be done by exercising self-control. This is the real distinction between a physical and moral life. This is also the primary basis for character. Character exhibits itself in control of speech as much as in anything else. It is necessary for one's own happiness to exercise control over his words as well as his acts for there are words that strike even harder than blows, and a person may "speak daggers" even though they use none. A wise person will restrain his desire to say a smart or harsh thing at the expense of another's feelings.

Self-control is a virtue that will become ours if we cultivate it properly. One exercise of it will not win us the victory. Victory comes only by constant repetition of efforts.

When the virtue of self-control is established early in life, it insures health, freedom from pain, competency, respectability, honor, usefulness, and happiness.

COURAGE

Courage consists not in hazarding without fear, but being resolute in a just cause. True courage is cool and calm. Rage can make a coward forget himself and fight. But what is done in fury or anger can never be called courage. Courage enlarges resources while cowardice diminishes them. For cowards the road to desertion should be kept open. They will carry over to the enemy nothing but their fears.

To believe something impossible is the way to make it so. How many feasible projects have miscarried through despondency, and been strangled in the birth by a cowardly imagination! Those who fear defeat are half conquered. Confront difficulties with unflinching perseverance. Should you then fail, you will be honored; but shrink and you will be despised.

No one can tell who the heroes are, and who the cowards are, until some crisis comes to put us to the test. And no crisis puts us to the test that does not bring us up alone and single-handed to face danger. It is comparatively easy to make a rush with the multitude, even into the jaws of destruction. Armies can be picked from the gutters. But when some crisis singles one out from the multitude while telling him, "Stand or run"—if he faces it with a steady nerve, we may be sure the hero stuff is in him. When such crises come, true courage is just as likely to be found in people thought to be weak and timid as in big and strong people. It is a moral, not a physical trait.

Some people imagine that courage is confined to the field of battle. There could be no greater mistake. There are other struggles with adverse circumstances—struggles with habits, appetites or passions—all of which require as much courage and more perseverance than the brief encounter of battle. There is enough to contend with and overcome every day in the pathway of every individual.

The greater part of the courage that is needed in the world is not the heroic kind. There needs to be the courage to be honest, the courage to resist temptation, the courage to speak the truth, the courage to be who we really are, and not pretend to be who we are not. A person must have the courage to be himself and not the shadow or the echo of another. He must think his own thoughts, elaborate his own opinions, and form his own convictions.

The passive endurance of the man or woman who for conscience sake is ready to suffer and endure in solitude, without the encouragement of even a single sympathizing voice, is an exhibition of courage of a far higher kind than that displayed in the roar of battle, where even the weakest feels encouraged and inspired by the enthusiasm and power of numbers. Time would fail to tell all the names of those who in the face of difficulties, dangers, and sufferings, have fought a good fight in the moral warfare of the world, and been content to lay down their lives rather than prove false to their convictions of the truth.

We must behave with dignity whether we are blessed or afflicted. We must not lose heart, or it will be worse both for ourselves and for those whom we love.

To struggle, and yet again and again renew the conflict, *this* is real courage.

⚜

COMPASSION

Compassion, like the dew from heaven that falls gently on drooping flowers in the stillness of night, is refreshing and its reviving effects are felt, seen, and admired. It flows from a good heart and looks beyond this world for approval and reward.

Compassion is another name for love—the humane, sympathetic feeling that seeks the good of others. It is the Good Samaritan of the heart. It seeks to heal

110

the wounds inflicted by misfortune. It thinks no evil and is kind. It hopes all things, believes all things, and endures all things. It forgives seventy and seven times, and is still rich in the treasures of pardon. It visits the sick, soothes the pillow of the dying, drops a tear with the mourner, buries the dead, and cares for the orphan. It delights to do good to those cast down, relieves the suffering of the oppressed and distressed and proclaims the gospel to the poor. Without the exercise of this virtue it is impossible to make domestic and social life delightful.

Whoever would be respected, beloved, and remembered with pleasure when life is over, must cherish this virtue. It is as boundless as the wants and needs of all creation. It is needed everywhere, in all times and places, in all trades, professions and callings which anyone can pursue. The peace and happiness of the world depends greatly upon it.

He who always carries with him the spirit of compassion often does good even without knowing it. The compassionate soul carries with it a charmed atmosphere of peace and love where the harsh discipline of life is changed to wholesome training, where crooked paths are made straight, and rough paths are made smooth.

In no other person do we find compassion more happily exemplified than in the life of our Savior, who, while on earth, "went about doing good."

KINDNESS

Kindness is one of the purest traits of the human heart. It makes sunshine and gives us friends wherever we go.

To show kindness, it is not necessary to give large sums of money, or to perform some wonderful deed that will immortalize your name. It is the tear dropped with the mother as she weeps over her departed child, the word of sympathy to the discouraged and disheartened, the cup of cold water and the slice of bread to the hungry one. A person may give money, which comes from the pocket or purse, and withhold kindness, which comes from the heart. Kindness comes from a gentle and generous spirit.

If you want others to remember you after you have passed away, write your name on the tablets of their hearts by acts of kindness, love, and mercy.

We should not permit ease and indulgence to lessen our affection and wrap us up in selfish enjoyment. Rather, we should think of the distresses of others and how to relieve them. It is the kind individuals who are active in the world, while the selfish and the skeptical love only themselves and are idle.

Little nameless acts of kindness and love are the best portion of a good person's life and they do much to increase the happiness of one's life. They drive away sadness and cheer up the soul. When administered in times of need they will be long remembered.

Words of kindness fitly spoken are worth much and cost little. Speak kindly in the morning for it lightens all the cares of the day. Speak kindly at night for it may be that before dawn some loved one may finish his or her space of life, and it will be too late to ask forgiveness. Always leave home with kind words, for they may be your last.

The seeds of courtesy and kindness may be scattered around with so little trouble and expense that it seems strange that more do not endeavor to spread them abroad. We should not be discouraged if our kindness is unacknowledged. The absence of gratitude on the part of the receiver cannot destroy the inner peace and happiness that rewards the kindly act.

The noblest revenge we can take upon our enemies is to do them a kindness. To return malice for malice and injury for injury will give us only temporary gratification, and our enemies will only be rendered more and more bitter against us. But to take the first opportunity of showing how superior we are to them by doing them a kindness, or by rendering them a service, is the more honorable way. The sting of reproach will enter deeply into their souls and our triumph will frequently be complete, bringing repentant hearts to offer themselves at the shrine of friendship. A more glorious victory cannot be gained over another individual than when the injury began on his part, the kindness began on ours.

Be generous with kind words and pleasing acts, for such gifts gladden the heart and sweeten the life of all who hear and receive them. They are jewels beyond price, powerful to heal the wounded heart, and make the weighed-down spirit glad.

~~❦~~

BENEVOLENCE

Only those who have experienced it can understand the joy resulting from the spreading of blessings to those around us. Doing good is the only certain happy action of a person's life. Never did any soul do good but he came readier to do the same again with more enjoyment. We do the most for ourselves when we do most for others; hence our highest interests, even from a purely selfish point of view, are the paths of benevolence. After all, we know it is "more blessed to give than to receive."

A true spirit of giving doesn't always mistrust the truth of the necessities revealed to it. Don't be frightened by the word "imposter." It is better to be sometimes mistaken than not to exercise charity at all. Though we might possibly give to the unworthy, it does not take away from the merit of the act. Some have unknowingly entertained angels.

A person may have a generous feeling for the welfare of the whole world, but he should have a preference for that particular part of the world in which he lives. Charity begins at home, but it may and *ought* to go abroad.

By aspiring to be like God in power, the angels fell; by aspiring to be like God in knowledge, man fell; but by aspiring to be like God in goodness or love, there is no transgression, for we are all called to that imitation.

Generosity during life is very different from generosity in the hour of death. One proceeds from genuine liberality and benevolence, the other from pride or fear. He that will not permit his wealth to do any good to others while he is living prevents it from doing any good to himself when he is gone. He surrenders everything when he sees he cannot continue to keep possession. The truly generous person does not wish to leave enough to build an imposing monument. He enjoys the pleasure that is his by giving it when alive and seeing others benefited.

In no heart is benevolence more beautiful than in youth and in no heart is selfishness more ugly. To *do* good is honorable; to *be* good is more honorable. This should be the aim of all those who are young. The poor and needy should occupy a large place in their hearts.

VERACITY

Without this virtue, there is no reliance upon language, no confidence in friendship and no security in promises and oaths. The love of truth and what is right is the source of integrity.

Truth is always consistent with itself, and needs nothing to help it out. It sits upon our lips ready to drop out before we are aware. A lie is troublesome, and one trick needs many more to make it good. Falsehood is difficult to maintain. When the materials of a building are solid stone, very crude architecture will suffice; but a structure of rotten materials needs the most careful adjustments to make it stand at all.

Strict observance of the truth requires something more than merely speaking the truth. There are lying looks as well as lying words and even a lying silence. You may pretend to concur with others' opinions and assume an attitude of conformity that is deceptive. You may make promises or allow them to be implied which are never intended to be kept or refrain from speaking the truth when it is your duty. There are also those who try to be all things to all people, who say one thing and do another. But those who are insincere discover that they have only deceived themselves while thinking they were deceiving others.

Denying a fault always doubles it. No wrong is ever made better, but always made worse, by a lie.

All that a person accomplishes by lying is that he will not be believed when he speaks the truth.

We are not called upon to speak all that we know; that would be folly. But what a person says should be what he thinks. While all we tell should be the truth, it is not always necessary to tell all the truth, unless the other one has a right to know. Silence is always an alternative with truth. Remember the silken cords of love must ever be linked to those of truth.

The person who forgets a great deal that has happened has a better memory than he who remembers a great deal that never happened.

Falsehood that baits her hook with truth and opinions that are not wholly wrong can fatally mislead us. No watch so effectively deceives the wearer as one that is sometimes right.

There is no virtue that doesn't originate in truth and there is no vice that doesn't begin in a lie.

～◎ ✿ ◎～

CONTENTMENT

A contented mind sees something good in everything and in every wind sees a sign of fair weather. A discontented spirit distorts all things, resolutely refusing to see anything but ill in its surroundings.

Nearly everyone we meet wishes to be what he is not, and every man thinks his neighbor's lot is happier than his own. He is complaining about his condition or finding fault with his particular calling. "If I were only this or that or the other, I would be content and happy," is the universal cry. Open the door to one discontented wish and you know not how many will follow.

The sailor envies the landsman; the landsman goes to sea for pleasure. The businessman who has to travel wishes for the day when he can "settle down," while the sedentary man is always wanting a chance to travel, which he thinks would be his greatest pleasure. Town people think the country is glorious while country people are always wishing that they might live in town.

Few are the real wants of a person. The majority of troubles are more imaginary than real. Enjoy the blessings if God sends them, and the evils bear patiently and sweetly. Something good can always be found regardless of how hopeless a situation seems. Providence has so ordered things that in every person's cup, no matter how bitter, there are some cordial drops—some good circumstances— which, if wisely extracted, are sufficient to make him contented. Strive to discover the pleasures and happiness to be found in your present condition and dwell therein until providence opens a more excellent way.

Contentment often abides with little, and rarely dwells with abundance. When you feel dissatisfied with your circumstances, contemplate the condition of those who have less than you.

One who wielded as much influence as was possible in this republic of ours says; "There are minds that can be pleased by honors and preferments, but I can see nothing in them save envy and enmity. It is only necessary to possess them to know how little they contribute to happiness. I had rather be in a cottage with my books, my family, and a few old friends, dining upon simply beans and bacon, and letting the world roll on as it likes, than to occupy the highest place which human power can give."

While true contentment bids you to be content with what you have and cheerfully accept the facts of your position, if the way opens for improvement, accept it at once. True contentment does not rest satisfied, hoping for nothing, striving for nothing, or doing nothing for your own or other's intellectual or moral good. So, don't make the mistake of hiding your lack of energy behind the word contentment.

Whoever desires the jewel of contentment must come with minds divested of all ambitious and covetous thoughts, or they are never likely to obtain it. The foundation of contentment must originate in a person's own mind. If a person seeks happiness by changing anything but his own disposition, he will waste his life in fruitless efforts.

POLITENESS

There is no virtue more underrated, especially by the young, than courtesy—that kindness and love which expresses itself in pleasing manners. In literature it is often the delicate charm of style that makes a work immortal. Likewise, it is the presentation and manner of a person that oftentimes promotes or obstructs his advancement in life. Good manners are the outward expression of inward virtue.

The *way* a person says or does something furnishes the best indicator of his character. One may do certain deeds from design, or repeat certain professions by memory. Honeyed words may mask feelings of hate, and kindly acts may be formed expressly to veil sinister ends, but the "manner" of the person is not so easily controlled.

An attractive manner is developed in years, not moments. It is the fruit of earnest, kindly endeavors to please. It is the last touch, the crowning perfection of an honorable character.

Nothing will develop a spirit of true politeness like a mind saturated with goodness, fairness, and generosity. Manners are different in every country, but true politeness is the same everywhere. Never allow manners to become an imitation of politeness.

Politeness must know no classification; the rich and the poor alike must share in its benefits. The truly polite person is recognized by his regard for the rights and feelings of others, even in trivial matters. He puts on no airs, nor hints by word or manner that he deems himself better, wiser, or richer than any one around him. He is never "stuck up," looking down upon others because they don't have titles, honors, or social position equal to his own.

Politeness must be sincere, originating in the heart, or it will not make a lasting impression. One must think of others and study how to please them even at his own inconvenience. "Do unto others as you would have them do unto you"—the golden rule of life—is also the law of politeness and pays alike in cash and comfort.

SOCIABILITY

Some of the highest enjoyments of life come from social interaction. Where there is a free exchange of opinions and ideas, the mind is exercised and understanding improves.

Society has been compared to a heap of embers, that when placed together, glow with intense heat, an emblem of strength, happiness, and security. But if the embers are separated, they soon languish, darken, and expire. The person who quits on society is like the separate embers, dark, dead, and useless; they neither give nor receive heat, they neither love nor are beloved.

Society is the arena where the character is formed and studied. It is the school of human faith and trials. No man is made solely for himself, and no man is capable of living in the world totally independent of others. The wants and weaknesses of mankind render society necessary for their convenience, safety, and support. God has formed each person with different powers and faculties, and placed them in different circumstances, that they might be able to promote each other's good. Some are wiser, richer, and stronger than others so that they may direct the conduct, supply the wants, and bear the burdens of others.

We are not well enough acquainted with each other. We are not social enough. We are not found often enough at one another's houses.

A person may contemplate virtue in solitude, but it is worked out by its participation in society because whatever is good is better for being communicated. You cannot move people until you show yourself one among them. You cannot know their wants and needs until you have mingled with them. Unless you cast your lot with others socially, you are powerless to do good to others. Each of us should strive to make everyone around us see and feel a spirit of goodwill and to meet them on a plane of equality.

Many young people fail to understand that they are subject to social duties. They act as though the social machinery of the world was self-operating. They do not think it is necessary for them to devote either time or money to society. This disposition is thoroughly selfish, and is to be overcome by going where you are invited. Do not shrink from contact with anyone except those with bad morals.

Some people enter society with ease while others remain away. Such are likely to think that society has not fulfilled its duties to them, but all social duties are reciprocal. Society is far more likely to pay its dues to the individual than the individual to society. If you are content to be a beneficiary of society, to receive favors and bestow none, you have no business in the social circle to which you aspire.

If it is your manner to forego meeting others socially, there will certainly come a time when you will regret it. The human heart is like a millstone in a mill. When you put wheat under it, it turns and bruises the wheat into flour. If you put no wheat in it, it still grinds on, but it grinds itself away. In society the sorrows of others are the objects from which we extract the flour of love and kindness, but to the hermit from society his own sorrows have the effect to render him cold and selfish. A good heart wants someone to be kind to and it suffers most when deprived of association with others.

No person can reflect upon the constant stream of good that is perpetually flowing down to him from society without feeling his obligation to maintain and support it. It becomes all people to seek the general good of society in return for the benefits they receive from it.

AFFABILITY

Affability is the most beautiful attire that a man or woman can wear. It is worth far more as a means of winning favor than the finest clothes and jewels ever were.

Apart from its worth as an agreeable trait of character, affability is a valuable commodity. Everyone who has business to transact should add this to his or her stock in trade. It costs nothing, while vastly facilitating trade and profit. There are men and women who in their businesses make fortunes simply by their affable and polite manners. Their wares or services are no better than their competitors, but they are wise enough to know that whatever is to be done successfully must be done in a pleasing manner and with good will. Their acts appear to be based on the conviction that everybody may be made a friend, which is preferable to acting as if everybody were an intruder. They do not treat people as though they were in a hurry to be done with them, but as though they might be cultivated into an acquaintance and grow into a friend. The reason some people are successful where others fail is that they invite strangers to become friends simply by being courteous to them.

We seldom think how others may be wishing for some friendly recognition or how far with them a friendly handshake may go. The man or woman who is affable and kind will make friends wherever he or she goes. Each one of us should strive to meet those around us with kindness and good will with no distinction as to rank or wealth. Give to all a hearty grasp and a sunny smile. They send sunshine to the soul, and make the heart leap as with new life and joy.

OUTER ADORNMENT

We believe it is the duty of all, young and old, to make themselves agreeable to those with whom they are associated, and it should be remembered that the dress should suit the time and occasion. If possible, dress yourself fine where others are fine, and plain where the apparel of others is plain. A person who finds himself badly dressed among well-dressed people feels awkward and ill at ease. However, the man in his work-shop or field, or the lady busy doing household chores in her own home, should not feel ill at ease because they are not dressed as finely as the casual caller. Such a feeling should be checked, since it is born of pride, not of an innate desire to please others.

Let no woman suppose that any man, much less her husband, is indifferent to her appearance. A woman's dress and adornments express her nature. When women are free to dress as they like, uncontrolled by others and not limited by their circumstances, they do not fail to express their true characters.

To advise a young lady to dress herself with any serious departure from the prevailing fashion of her day is to advise her to incur a penalty which may very well wreck her whole life's happiness.

Dressing to be in perfect taste need not be costly. A woman of good sense will not wish to spend in unnecessary extravagance money wrung from an anxious husband. In the early years of married life, when the income is moderate, it should be the pride of the woman to see how little she can spend upon her dress and yet present that tasteful appearance which she desires.

It is unfortunate that both men and women fail to recognize the beauty that always accompanies simplicity. Gold and diamonds cannot compensate for the absence of true taste and refinement. Those who think that in order to dress well it is necessary to dress extravagantly or gaudily make a great mistake. Elegance of dress does not depend upon expense, for without grace, it is nothing.

It must be remembered that outward adornment should be secondary to the adornment of the soul with all other virtuous qualities.

❦

MEMORY

Without memory, life would be a blank, unlettered page. Memory has been compared to a vast storehouse. Affections that apparently came to an end and dropped out of life one way or another were only lying dormant. A scent, a song, a voice long unheard, or the stirring of a summer breeze may startle us with sudden revival of long forgotten feelings and thoughts.

The man or woman who is able to recall the direction and counsel of a wise father and faithful mother will seldom act in an unworthy or unjust manner.

Our memory does not always conjure up thoughts that are joyous. In this sense, memory is a faithful steward that also allows us to remember scenes we wish we could forget. How important then it is to take into our mind healthful thoughts instead of feeding it on poisons until it will produce nothing but poisonous actions! Inasmuch as the mind derives much of its pleasures from thoughts of the past, we should as far as possible provide for happy memories. This is the reward of right living.

Memory has a strange power of crowding years into moments. This is often observed when death is about to close the last scene of life. As the sunlight breaks from the clouds and across the hills at the close of a stormy day, lighting up the distant horizon, even so does memory break forth and illumine the most distant scenes and events of past years.

HAPPINESS

It is in the pursuit of happiness that the energies of man are put forth. Earthly happiness is a phantom. Anticipation is her herald, but disappointment is her companion. The anticipation of a pleasure may have lasted for weeks in the mind while the reality lasts but a short time. Hence the feeling of disappointment ensues. The ideal scene is painted in bright colors — there are no drawbacks or disappointments, but in reality they are sure to appear.

We may look for happiness in one direction, but find it in another, and sometimes where we least expect it. There is a fable in which a man told his sons of a hidden mass of wealth that he had buried in his vineyard. It led them to so carefully search the ground that they found a treasure, though not in gold, but in wine.

We are shortsighted, and fail to see the end of things. A great deal of the misery of life comes from the desire to have things our own way, as though we could not be happy under any circumstances except those we have framed to meet our own wants.

Circumstances are not half as essential to our happiness as most people imagine.

Because we cannot find happiness in our own way, we will not accept it in the appointed way. We lose sight of the fact that God rules above us and we live amid a multitude of influences we cannot altogether control. Nor is it best we should.

It is not for man wholly to determine his steps. Sometimes what he thinks is for his good turns out to be harmful; and what he thinks is unfavorable develops into a great blessing in disguise. It is folly to be miserable because things are not as we would have them. Many of our plans must be defeated for our own good.

Those who are so concerned about their outward circumstances are often affected by mere trifles. Molehills are magnified into mountains, and in the shadow of these mountains they sit down and weep. A little thing shadows their life for days. They cannot enjoy today because of the want of some convenience, some personal gratification, or some outward ornament. The very things they ought to have sometimes come unasked, and because they are not ready for them they will not enjoy them.

There is also a disposition in the minds of some to multiply their troubles as well as magnify them. They make troubles of many things that should be regarded as privileges, opportunities for self-sacrifice, or for improving effort. They make troubles of the ordinary allotments of life—its duties, changes, unavoidable accidents, reverses, and experiences. However, these are ordained by infinite wisdom as a healthy discipline for the soul of man.

Some spend life determined to be vastly happy at some future time, but for the present put off all enjoyment of passing pleasures, seemingly for fear that all such pleasures will detract from future enjoyments. Do not trample under foot the little pleasures that a gracious God scatters in the daily path of life while you are searching for some great and exciting joy. It is in the daily duties of life while humbly seeking to do what is right that we unexpectedly find that for which are searching.

Happiness is much more equally divided than some of us imagine. It has been compared to the manna in the desert, "he that gathered much had nothing left over, and he that gathered little had no lack." Therefore, to diminish envy, let us consider not what others possess, but what they enjoy. We should enjoy the fruit of our labor while we have our health and vigor rather than laboring for possessions so vast and expensive that it costs us the best part of our lives.

In life we all seek happiness and success. When we admit that happiness is but a state of the mind, and that success is the faithful performance of known duties, then we shall acquire both.

The person who carries a lantern on a dark night can have friends walking safely along by the light of its rays, and not defraud himself. So he who has a cheerful disposition and the light of hope in his heart can help many others in this world's darkness, not to his own loss, but to their gain.

Let a cheerful word fall from your lips, and a smile play upon your face. Gather all the happiness out of life that you can. Strive to cultivate a cheerful and hopeful disposition that will enable you to see the silver lining to every cloud. By such a course you will do much to ease the sorrows and increase the joys and pleasures of life.

OPPORTUNITY

Many people are ready to suppose that they fail in life from a lack of those great occasions where they might have shown their trustworthiness and integrity. But in order to find whether a vessel is leaky we must first prove it with water before we trust it with wine. It is the proper employment of smaller opportunities that gives occasion to the great ones. It is one of the common mistakes of life to wait for opportunities.

A person's opportunity usually has some relation to his ability. If he says, "I want a better opportunity than that; I am worthy of a higher position than that," or if he thinks the opportunity is too insignificant to be embraced, he is very likely in later years to see the folly of his course. There are scores of young people who want to acquire wealth, and yet everyday reject such opportunities that our really rich men and women would have improved. They want to begin, not as others do, at the foot of the ladder, but half way up. Somehow they want to avoid the early and demanding struggles of those who have been successful.

The most unsuccessful people are usually the ones who think they could do great things if they only had the opportunity. They knew just how to get rich, but they lacked opportunity. A person cannot expect that great opportunities will meet him all along his life like milestones by the wayside. Usually he has one or two. A Roman cardinal said, "There is nobody whom fortune doesn't visit once in his life. But when she finds he is not ready to receive her, she goes in at the door and out through the window."

The real materials that form our characters are the hourly occurrences of everyday life. If we watch through a single day we shall doubtless discover hundreds of opportunities of both doing and receiving good. We must be alert to discover opportunities and take advantage of them. To the feeble, the sluggish, the purposeless, opportunities avail nothing. They pass them by, seeing no meaning in them. But to the energetic, wide-awake person, they are great moments that may be improved and contribute in no small degree to his or her ultimate success.

VICES TO AVOID

VANITY

There is no vice or folly that requires so much nicety and skill to manage as vanity, or if ill managed, makes so contemptible a figure.

People are more likely to be vain on account of those qualities that they fondly believe they have rather than of those that they really possess. The desire of being thought wise is often a hindrance to being so. Such a person is often trying to show the world the knowledge he has rather than learn from others the wisdom he so desires.

In the same degree we overrate ourselves we tend to underrate others. A person should not prize himself by what he has; neither should others prize him by what he professes to have. It is a mistake to value a jewel by its golden frame or a book by its cover or a person by what he professes.

The person who is greedy for popular applause should remember that the same breath that blows up a fire may blow it out again.

The rich and poor, learned and ignorant, strong and weak, all have a share of vanity. It is so anchored in the heart of man that all wish to have their admirers.

God will exalt the humble and humble the proud. If we have any good qualities, they are a gift of God.

SELFISHNESS

There is nothing in the world so destructive in its nature as selfishness. It has done all the mischief of the past, and is destined to do all the mischief of the unseen future. It is the source of all the sins of omission and commission that are found in the world. Every wrong that takes place happens because someone is moved by his own private, personal, and selfish nature.

The selfish person lives as if the world were made altogether for him, and not he for the world — to be a taker rather than a giver. He tends to think only of himself in all things. The person who falls in love with himself will have no rivals.

There are some people whose opposition can be counted upon against every thing that doesn't originate with them. It is by reason of their selfishness that they find the world so ugly, because they can only see themselves in it.

Often we dislike selfishness in others simply because of our own. We feel it a slight when someone talks about himself and tries to entertain us with his own interests instead of asking us about ours. He who thinks he can do without others is mistaken. But he who thinks others cannot do without him is even more mistaken.

If all our thoughts, plans, and purposes are for the advancement of self, we will fail to attract others to our causes.

Selfishness takes from a person that feeling of kindly sympathy for another's good and in its place sets up self as the one whose good in mainly sought. It contracts and narrows our benevolence. As frost is to the bud, self-interest is to friendship, for confidence cannot dwell where selfishness is the keeper of the gate.

The closing hours of a life of selfishness must be clouded with many painful thoughts. Chances for doing good passed unimproved. The heart, which was intended to beat with compassion for others, has become contracted to a narrow circle, and passes on to the next world unprepared for the great changes brought about by the hand of death.

Selfishness is a vice utterly at variance with the happiness of the person who harbors it. He that shares in the happiness of others enjoys the safest happiness, and he who is warned by the folly of others has attained the soundest wisdom.

STUBBORNNESS

Sometimes stubbornness is confused with perseverance, which is considered a virtue. But the difference is distinctive. Perseverance, while not easily driven from its course, recognizes that for things imperfect, change is a way to improve them. Stubbornness is a barrier to improvements because it will not submit to a change for the better. Stubbornness declines to listen to reason, and prevents us from acknowledging the truth that is perfectly plain to everyone else.

Whoever resolves to adhere to plans or opinions, whether they are right or wrong, just because they have adopted them, raises an impassable bar to information. There is no virtue that requires us to continue in our former course when convinced it is wrong. Narrow-mindedness is often the cause of stubbornness; we do not easily believe beyond what we see. Stubbornness denotes a dwarfed, ignorant, and selfish disposition.

Those who have just entered the vestibule of the temple of knowledge invariably feel themselves much wiser than those who meekly worship in the inner sanctuary. Being absolutely sure about a matter is much more apt to accompany the statement of the superficial observer than the person whose experience has been vast and profound. The wiser we are the more we are aware of the extent of our ignorance.

There are situations in which the proper mode of action isn't evident. In such cases, we must maturely seek the opinions of others wiser and better acquainted with the subject than ourselves. Only then can we hope to decide wisely. A person who is not willing to give way at times to the wishes of others will forgo much happiness.

SLANDER

It is silly to value yourself based upon the opinions of others. Never depend on what others say about you for peace in your life. When someone speaks unfavorably of you, take it thus: If you have not deserved it, you are none the worse; if you have, then mend, for it is a just correction. Examine your own heart. Remember it is the best fruits that the birds pick at, and slanderers are like flies that overlook all a person's good parts in order to light upon his sores. The person who is never the subject of slander is generally of too little account to be worthy of it.

The tongue of slander is never tired. Sometimes it is bitter and sometimes sweet. It will hide a curse among smooth words and administer poison in phrases of love.

When a person is absent, say nothing to damage his reputation. He may be wrong and immoral, yet your knowledge of it does not oblige you to disclose his character, except to save others from harm. Then, do it in a spirit of kindness for the absent offender. He that indulges himself in ridiculing the absent plainly shows others what they may expect from him after he leaves them.

Evil reports are often the results of misunderstanding or they proceed from an exaggerated or partial disclosure of facts. Wait, learn the whole story, and then believe what the evidence compels you to and no more.

Slander is not long-lived, provided that your conduct doesn't justify it. Truth and time will vindicate you.

Never does a person portray his own character more vividly than the way he portrays another person's character. There is something unsound about the person whom you have never heard say a good word about anyone—who can say much evil of nearly all he is acquainted with. Never speak evil of another, even with a cause. Remember we all have our faults, and if we expect charity from the world we must be charitable ourselves.

Neither take pleasure in hearing ill of others. Give no heed to a story handed to you by a person known to be an enemy of the one he is defaming. Do not condemn your neighbor unheard, for there are always two sides of a story. Hear no ill of a friend, nor speak any of an enemy.

Remember that a word spoken can never be recalled; therefore it is prudent to think twice before we speak. The tongue of prudence knows when to speak and when to be silent. It dares to say all that need be said, but it does not tell all that it knows. It is careful *what* it speaks, *when* it speaks, and *to whom* it speaks. There are sad inscriptions deeply engraved by the tongue of slander on hearts and minds which no effort can erase. They are more durable than the impressions a diamond leaves on glass, for the inscription on the glass may be destroyed by a blow, but the impression on the heart can last a lifetime.

May we guard our lips well so that none grieve in silence over words we have carelessly dropped. We must strive to scatter loving, cheering, encouraging words to those with whom we daily come in contact.

⚜

IRRITABILITY

The person who has the reputation of being irritable is repulsive and annoying to those with whom he comes into contact. Many who have much to be thankful for are full of complaint. Such a disposition is unfortunate and reprehensible. They make miserable not only their own life, but also the lives of those they are around every day.

Irritable people are always unjust, always exacting, and always dissatisfied. They expect everything of others, and yet receive their best efforts with disdain. This habit has an unfortunate tendency to grow until it renders a person wholly incapable of conferring happiness upon others.

Let a person get the reputation of being touchy, and everybody is under restraint in his or her presence. The people who are easily angered miss a great deal of happiness in life. They always have some fancied slight to brood over. Sunny, serene moments never visit them.

Irritability is a vain and useless habit. It sours a person's disposition and breaks up friendships. An irritable disposition will find frequent opportunities for indulgence. It isn't particular as to time, place, or cause. Nothing seems to go right for the possessor of this vice.

An irritable person is selfish and cares for no one but himself. He will not defer to the wishes of others in the slightest degree. It is far wiser to take a more charitable view of our fellow men.

***

ENVY

Envy is the daughter of Pride and the author of murder and revenge. Like a worm, it prefers the best fruits; like a bloodhound, it singles out the fattest deer in the herd.

The envious person is in pain upon all occasions that ought to give him pleasure. He laments over another's prosperity, youth, beauty, valor, and wisdom. The envious person is tormented not only by all the ills that befall him, but also by all the good that happens to another. Whoever feels pain in learning good of his neighbor will feel pleasure in the reverse.

Envy is a sentiment that desires to equal, or excel, the accomplishments of its peers, not so much by increasing our own toil and ingenuity as by diminishing the merits of other's achievements. It detests the sound of another's praise, and deems no renown acceptable that must be shared. The person who works to rise above average and who does his duty well, must realize that part of his reward will be hatred from some of his peers.

Envy is not confined to any rank of people or extent of fortune. We are as apt to find it in the humble walks of life as in the proud, as much in the young as in the aged. We must watch for it in all its disguises so that we may dislodge it before it finds a shelter to conceal itself and work to our detriment and shame.

⚜

JEALOUSY

It is difficult sometimes to distinguish between jealousy and envy, for they often run into one another and are blended together. The most valid distinction seems to be that jealousy is always personal. The envious man desires some good that another possesses; the jealous man suspects another of seeking to deprive him of some good that he already possesses. Jealousy is preferable to envy since it aims at the preservation of some good that we think belongs to us, whereas envy is a frenzy that cannot endure the good of others.

Jealousy is dangerous because it is a headstrong passion. It looks facts straight in the face, ignores them, and says she knows a great deal better than they can tell her.

Jealousy violates contracts, breaks wedlock, and betrays friends and neighbors. It is a vain and foolish pride that causes you to believe that everyone is conspiring against your happiness or has designs on your reputation and business. The fact is, probably no one is thinking of you. Yet your jealous disposition magnifies every little circumstance, and causes you to be unhappy when no real cause exists.

In nothing is jealousy more commonly shown than in the fear that someone will supplant us in the affections of another. When one treasures and trusts a woman's love and is deceived, hope is gone, and it is difficult to find again. Do not too strictly judge a jealous woman or a jealous man. Remember that they suffer from selfishness, often without a shadow of a cause; but still it is suffering, and it is intense.

It is said that jealousy is love. This is not true; for jealousy extinguishes love, as ashes smother the flame. In fact, jealousy commonly exists without love, for jealousy can feed on that which is bitter or on that which is sweet, and is sustained by pride as often as by affection.

Jealousy injures and pains no one as much as the person feeling it. It is a self-consuming fire, a self-inflicted torment. Of all passions, there is not one that has a vision more distorted or a more unreasonable fury. There is no passion that seeks to hide itself more than jealousy and it is ashamed of itself when it appears.

DECEPTION

Deceit and falsehood, whatever conveniences they may for a time promise or produce, are in reality obstacles to happiness. The origin of deceit is always found in the motives of those who are thoroughly selfish. When a person has some personal end to accomplish, some enemy or rival to punish, then deceit is seen in full bloom.

Deceit that is cunningly carried on under the disguise of friendship is, above all others, the most detestable. Nothing can be more unjust than to play upon the trust of a confiding person, and then make him suffer for thinking you are an honest person.

People are naturally set on ambition, as bees are to gather honey. In the mad haste to stand well in the eyes of the public, they are prone to assume any disguise or counterfeit any virtue by which they may accomplish their selfish ends. They are more concerned by the outward and external effects of an evil course of life than by the evil itself.

Is it not true that "honesty is the best policy?" Why purchase the base imitation of noble virtues, and derive from them nothing but ridicule and dislike, when no greater outlay would procure for us the true metals, which bring peace of mind and the honor and esteem of all.

━◉ ⚜ ◉━

INTERMEDDLING AND GOSSIP

All of us scorn a busybody, that is, one who is constantly meddling in matters that in no way concerns him. As soon as one discovers some failure or fault, he can't wait to tell others the fruits of his investigation. And thus is given to the public the petty defects of some home life, which by constant repetition assumes gigantic size, and the happiness of some home circle is destroyed by malicious busybodies. A person who constantly meddles means to do harm, and is not sorry to find he has succeeded.

The less business a person has of his own, the more he attends to the business of his neighbors. Neglecting our own affairs and meddling with those of others is the source of many troubles. Those who blow the coals of others' strife risk having the sparks fly in their own face. People are often incited to meddle by the desire of having "something to tell." But, if you notice, they are narrow-minded and ignorant people, who talk about people and not things. Mere gossip is always a personal confession of malice, and you should shun it and avoid all temptation to indulge in it. It is a low, frivolous, and often a dirty business. Churches are split in pieces by it; neighbors are made enemies by it for life. In many people it degenerates into a chronic disease that is practically incurable. Be on your guard against contracting such a habit.

There is not a more detestable character in the world than a go-between—the person who carries to the ear of a neighbor every injurious observation that happens to drop from the mouth of another. Such a person is the slanderer's herald. He makes that poison effective which otherwise would be inert; for three-fourths of the slanderers in the world would never injure their objects except by the malice of go-betweens, who under the mask of a double friendship, act the part of a double traitor.

Every person has in his own life follies enough, in

146

his own mind troubles enough, in the performance of his own duties difficulties enough, without being curious about the affairs of others. The curiosity of the meddler isn't directed toward discovering where he can lend a helping hand. If such were the case, it would be a trait to be admired rather than despised. The curiosity of an honorable person willingly ceases where the love of truth does not urge it further onward, and the love of his neighbor bids it stop.

If one wants to be honored and respected, he will strive to be as free from the spirit of meddling as possible. He will relegate that to the low and frivolous, and respect himself too highly to be classed among them.

ANGER

Consider how much more you suffer from your anger than from those things for which you are angry. Anger hurts the person who is possessed by it more than the person against whom it is directed. In moments of cool reflection the person who indulges in anger views with deep disgust the desolation caused by it.

Friendship, domestic happiness, self-respect, and the esteem of others are swept away by one brief fit of anger. On occasion, it suffices to wreck the happiness in a home that took years to cement together.

A passionate temper renders a person unfit for advice or conversation. It deprives him of reason, changes justice into cruelty, and turns order into confusion. Crimes are committed in the passion of anger.

There are times and occasions when the expression of indignation is not only justifiable, but necessary. We are bound to be indignant at falsehood, selfishness, cruelty, baseness or meanness of any sort. But, the sword of reproof should be drawn against the offense and not against the offender.

Anger glances off the breast of a wise man, but rests in the bosom of fools.

When anger becomes strong, it is called wrath; when it makes outrage, it is fury; when it becomes fixed, it is termed hatred; and when intended to injure someone, it is called malice. The intoxication of anger, like that of the grape, shows us to others, but conceals us from ourselves. We injure our own cause in the eyes of the world when we too passionately and eagerly defend it.

There are some people who might govern multitudes if they could only govern their own tongue. When does someone feel more at ease with himself than when he has passed through a sudden and strong provocation without speaking a word and still possesses undisturbed good humor? When, on the other hand, does he feel a deeper humiliation than when he is conscious that anger has made him betray himself? How many are able to check passion with passion?

It is not the falling into the water, but remaining in it that drowns a person. So it is not the possession of a strong and hasty temper, but the submission to it, that produces the evils incident to it. A strong temper subjected to the guiding reins of self-control renders success in any endeavor not only possible, but probable.

AMBITION

The history of ambition is written in characters of blood. It is a vice of small minds unacquainted with mankind. It is a solitary vice. The road ambition travels is too narrow for friendship, too crooked for love, too rugged for honesty, and too hilly for happiness.

The happiness promised by ambition dissolves in sorrow just as we are about to grasp it. She begins by accumulating power as a means to happiness, but she finishes by continuing to accumulate it as an end.

A thoroughly ambitious person will never make a true friend, for he who makes ambition his god tramples upon everyone else. It matters not to him if he treads upon the hearts of those who love him most. In his eyes your only value lies in the use you may be to him. If you are not rich or famous or powerful enough to advance his interests, after he has gotten above you, he cares no more for you.

Ambition makes people liars and cheats. Like fire, ambition is an excellent servant, but a poor master. If it is made to conform to the requirements of justice, there is little danger of a person having too much of it. But beware! You must be continually on your guard lest it speedily becomes the ruling principle of your being.

A worthy aspiration may be a great incentive to the advancement of civilization, and a great teacher of morality and wisdom. But an unworthy ambition, unworthy because of its ends or the zeal with which it is pursued, is often the instrument of crime and injustice.

Much of the advancement of the world can be traced to the efforts of those who were moved by ambition to become famous. But, it is a troublesome ambition that cares too much about what the world says about us—to always be looking for the approval of others. What profit will it be to us a year from now when other names are clamored for louder than ours?

But if we are ambitious to do good, without any regard for fame or praise, our course will be honorable and just. When we leave this world the rewards of our worthy ambition will still remain as a legacy for those who come after us to enjoy and benefit from. They will revere our memory, and retain our names in the lists of those whose labors have aided in enriching the world and exalting the interests of mankind.

TRIALS OF LIFE

TRIALS

In the changes of real life, joy and grief are never far apart. A wedding party returns from church, and a funeral train leaves from the adjacent house. Laughter and tears are twin-born.

Life that is all sunshine and no shade, all happiness without sorrow, all pleasure without pain, is not life at all. Life is made up of joys and sorrows, and the joys are all the sweeter because of the sorrows.

We should always remember that the trials of life are sent for our good and our instruction. God knows what keys in the human soul to touch in order to draw out its sweetness. Do not think that uninterrupted joy is good. The sunshine lies upon the mountaintop all day, and lingers there latest and longest at sunset. Yet it is the valley that is green and fertile, while the peak is barren and unfruitful.

Trials come in a thousand different forms, and many avenues are open to their approach. They come in our youth, in our adulthood, and depart not from the descending footsteps of old age. You may be so old that ambition has no charm, but you are never too old to experience trials.

A person's character is disciplined by trials and made perfect through suffering. As some herbs need to be crushed to give forth their sweetest odors, so some natures need to be tried by suffering to evoke the excellence that is in them. Some natures are like grapes—the more they are downtrodden the richer tribute they supply.

Afflictions are the nursery of virtue. They have the effect of eliciting talents that in prosperous circumstances would have remained dormant. How can we exercise the grace of contentment if all things succeed or that of forgiveness if we have no enemies?

Some of the saddest experiences of life come without warning. Yesterday life went well. It was easy to be content. Today all is reversed. The crushed heart can scarcely lift itself to pray. Speech seems paralyzed. It seems cruel that such calamity should be permitted, when we might have been so happy. Was there not some way by which it could have been avoided? What are ambitions worth in the face of this?

When God sees fit to afflict, we should not complain of oppression, but, with submission and love, perform the duties of life. When sorrow and grief come, we must not let darkness obscure the talents that God has given us to promote our own and other's happiness, or bury them with the brighter past, but nobly use them. To bear the ills of life patiently is one of the noblest virtues.

A person cannot just gaze at the beautiful sword in the shop window and know the process by which it was perfected. We are like the blade, daily life is the workshop, God is the craftsman, and the trials and sorrows of life are the very things that fashion us.

Never meet trouble halfway, but let him have to walk the whole way for his pains. Perhaps he will give up on his visit even in sight of your house. Do not declare that God has forsaken you when your way is hedged about with thorns, when trials and troubles meet you on every side. No person's life is free from struggles, not even the happiest.

Everyone may build up his own happiness by making himself independent of outward fortune. If misfortune comes, be patient and remember that he will soon leave because he cannot bear cheerful company. Happy are those who are able to pass through trials with cheerfulness and stand erect beneath the heaviest burdens.

Calamity never leaves us where it finds us. It either softens or hardens the heart of its victim. The same furnace that hardens clay, liquifies gold. Misfortune is never mournful to the soul that accepts it. The simplest and most obvious use of sorrow is to remind us of God. We are not conscious of breathing until obstruction makes it felt. God says to the fruit tree "bloom and bear" and to the human heart "bear and bloom." The soul's great blooming is the flower of suffering. As the sun converts clouds into a glorious drapery, firing them with gorgeous hues, so sometimes a radiant heart shines forth its hopes upon its sorrows.

The difficulties, hardships, and trials of life—the obstacles one encounters on the road to fortune— are positive blessings. All difficulties come to us, as Bunyan says of temptation, like the lion that met Sampson. The first time we encounter them they roar and gnash their teeth, but once subdued we find a nest of honey in them. Power is developed in the midst of peril. Opposition is what we want and must have to be good for anything.

In the trials of life we must look more for consolation within than without. The surest consolations of life are those that we derive from our own thoughts. The thoughts of the mind should go out and reach after higher good. In this manner we may improve ourselves until our thoughts come to be sweet companions leading us along the paths of virtue. Thus we may grow better within and the cares of life, the losses and disappointments, lose their sharp thorns and the journey of life is made comparatively pleasant and happy.

REGRET

"For of all sad words of tongue or pen,
The saddest are these, `It might have been.'"
--Whittier

There is not a word in the English language that expresses sorrow more than the word regret. This is especially true in the remorse a person feels when the sands of life are almost run out and he contemplates a wasted life. However, no age escapes regret and such will ever be the case as long as it is human to err.

The profoundest sorrow is not brought upon us by the world, by its bitterness, its malice, its injustice or its persecution. We can, if we choose, repel the world's wrongs. It is when we experience the sorrows brought upon ourselves by our own lack of discretion or stubbornness that we begin to understand what real sorrow is. There is added force to sorrow when we reflect that we are to blame, that we knew at the time that we were doing wrong, that we disregarded the warning voice of conscience and rejected the advice of others, that we are harvesting sorrow sown by our own negligence. We cannot repel its attacks with indifference.

While regret is the heart's sorrow for past offenses, it is also the soul's prompting to better actions. Heed the warning voice of reflection. Have you ever stood by the grave of one dear to you, and thought how much happier you might have made that life which has now passed beyond your reach? Let one of your loved ones be taken away, and memory recalls a thousand regrets. A man never sees so far into human life as when he looks over a wife's or a mother's grave. His eyes get wondrously clear then, and he sees as never before what it is to love and be loved, what it is to injure the feelings of the beloved.

To escape regret, avoid impulsive actions. Pause before you say a hasty or cruel thing. Has the hasty or unkind word ever come back to you and repeated itself over and over, until you would gladly have given a year of your own life to have recalled it and made it as if it had never been? Pause before acting in a hasty or inconsiderate manner. You may not be able to undo its effects. Human life is so uncertain. Are you sure you will have a chance to make it right before death claims the person you have wronged?

When one has done the best he can, he should let that fact console him, and not give way to causeless regret and wish that he had done differently.

Under the guiding light of the present it is easy enough to discover the mistakes of the past; and it would be easy to make advantageous changes were we allowed to go back and commence anew in the journey of life. But that is not possible! We should learn from the lessons of the past so that we become fully fitted for the duties of the present.

Regret, if deep and hopeless, becomes remorse, which settles down over the heart with a crushing weight, driving away all hope. It may be the sorrow of a reputation gone, or some act of folly that swept away the good name founded on years of honest living. Perhaps it is the shadow of a grave dark and deep, which covers the form of one which death claimed before we had made right some careless wrong done. Hasty and inconsiderate marriages cause much regret. The happiness of life is gone; the hopes of a home and an endearing companionship are gone because hasty action was taken where care and study was required.

Of all regrets, the remorse that accompanies the closing moments of a misspent life possesses the sharpest sting. Oh, that the young would listen and heed the warning voice of experience, and thus escape the regrets of later years!

How are you spending your life? Are you striving to make the most of life and its possibilities? If not, be warned and turn from your ways. When life is nearly ended you will think of the past, wonder at your actions, and sigh for the days of youth. They will not come to you again. Therefore, make the most of them *now*. Then you will spare yourself many vain regrets, and your closing days will be days of peace.

PROSPERITY

Prosperity is a great test of human character and not many are able to endure it. If prosperity carries a person ever so little beyond his poise, it can destroy him.

When the heart has no more to wish for, it yawns over its possessions, and the energy of the soul goes out like a flame that has no more to devour. A smooth sea never made skillful mariners; neither do uninterrupted prosperity and success qualify a person for usefulness and happiness. The storms of adversity, like those of the ocean, rouse our faculties and excite invention, prudence, and skill on the voyage thru life.

Adversity in early life often lays the foundation for future prosperity. The hand of adversity is cold, but it is the hand of a friend. As a wise man once said, "He that begins where his father ends will generally end where his father began."

The patient conquest of difficulties which arise in the regular and legitimate channels of business and enterprise is not only essential in securing the ultimate prosperity you seek, but also serves to prepare your mind for enjoying your prosperity. Everywhere in the human experience, as in nature, hardship is essential to ultimate success. The magnificent oak may be detained twenty years in its upward growth while its roots take a great turn around a bolder, which anchors the tree to withstand the storms of centuries.

Many make the mistake of supposing that prosperity and happiness are identical terms. However, the most prosperous are often the most miserable.

True prosperity is the result of a well-lived life that is rewarded with contentment. Its imitation is gained by unjust or dishonest means and cannot bring inner peace.

Those who are prosperous, or who have achieved greatness and notoriety in any pursuit, must expect to make enemies. Whoever becomes distinguished is sure to be a mark for the malicious spite of those who are infuriated by the merited triumph of those more worthy. On the other hand, opposition, if it is honest, is not necessarily undesirable.

Uninterrupted prosperity shows us but one side of the world. For, as it surrounds us with friends who will tell us only our merits, it also silences those enemies from whom we can learn our defects.

The earth cannot bask always in the sunshine. The snows and frosts of winter must come and work in the ground to make it fruitful. A person upon whom continuous sunshine falls is like the earth in

August--parched and hard. To some people the Winter comes when they are young. Others are born in Summer, and made fit to live only by a Winter of sorrow coming to them when they are middle-aged or old. But it must come, and the mind is fitted for the routine of life. Then the warm, shining sun of prosperity spreads abroad in the heart its quickening influence, and the best virtues of a person are developed.

The way to prosperity depends chiefly on two words —industry and frugality; that is, waste neither time nor money, but make the best use of both. Moderate prosperity is to be expected as the proper reward of life's exertion. Such prosperity, hopefully, will fill a person with the sweet juices of courtesy and charity, just as the sun ripens peaches and apricots.

TRIFLES

It is to the contempt of details that many people can trace the cause of their present misfortune. The world is full of those who languish, not from the lack of talents, but because they continually underestimate the value of trifles. Their soul is afire with lofty concepts of some work to be achieved, but when they begin to execute the plan, they turn away in disgust from the minutia and drudgery that are required for its accomplishment. It is all very well and good to form vast plans, however, it is the details of their execution that furnish the crucial tests of character. Failing to do the small tasks of life, they have no calling to higher ones.

It must be remembered that life is made up of trifles. As pennies make the dollar and minutes the hour, so it is the little details, mere trifles, that go to make success in any calling. In the majority of cases where people have failed, it was because they neglected little things deemed too microscopic to need attention. Steady attention to matters of detail is the mother of good fortune.

It is this attention to detail that makes the difference between the practical man, who pushes his thoughts to a useful result, and the mere dreamer. If we would do much good in the world, we must do the first good thing we can, and then the next. This is the only way to accomplish much in one's lifetime. He who waits to do a great deal of good at once will never do anything. Little sums make up the grand total of life. Great things seldom come and are often unrecognized until they are passed.

The disposition of mankind is to despise the little incidents of everyday life. This is a mistake, since nothing in this life is really small. It is strange on what petty trifles the crises of life are decided. A chance meeting with some friend or stranger, an unexpected delay in some business venture, may be the source from which you date your good or ill fortune.

If one undertakes to become rich, but despises the small and gradual advances by which wealth is ordinarily acquired, his expectations will be the sum of his riches.

The difference between first and second class work in every kind of labor lies chiefly in the care with which the details are executed.

Much of the unhappiness in life is caused by trifles. It is the petty annoyances of life, to be met and conquered afresh each day, that tests most severely the metal of which we are made. The great sorrows of life are mercifully few, but the innumerable petty ones of everyday occurrence cause many to grow weary of the burden of life.

The happiness of life is also largely composed of trifles. The occasions of great joys, like those of great sorrows, are few and far between, but every day brings us much good if we will but gather it.

LEISURE

Spare moments are the gold dust of time—the portion of life most fruitful for good or evil. When gathered up and used, important results flow from them; when neglected they are gaps through which temptation finds a ready entrance. They are a treasure when rightly used, but a terrible curse when abused.

We do not value time as we should. It is the most precious thing in the world. Time is so precious that there is never but one moment in the world at once, and that is always taken away before another is given.

When the young come into possession of an estate, it is rarely prized till it is nearly squandered. Likewise, when life is waning fast, it is then that one begins to think of spending the hours and moments wisely. But the habits of idleness and procrastination once firmly fixed cannot be suddenly thrown off, and the person who has wasted the precious hours of life's seedtime finds that he cannot reap a harvest in life's Autumn. This realization brings sadness as he ponders over wasted time—the hours he spent in a worse than foolish manner. It is only then that he understands the value of time. But alas! The lesson comes too late. Therefore, live wisely and consider the end of your existence. Reflect on the possibilities of life and resolve to waste no time in idleness.

It is astonishing what can be done when the determination is made to use leisure time rightly. Take care to gather up your fragments of leisure time, employ them judiciously, and you will find time for the accomplishment of almost any desired purpose—even undertakings that before seemed impossible.

Life is composed in such a way that whenever a duty is removed, the surrounding atmosphere of trifles rushes in as certainly as air into a bottle when you pour out its contents. If you don't want your hours of leisure frittered away on trifles you must guard them with resolute determination.

The people in any community who have done the most good are not the wealthy, leisurely people who have nothing to do, but are almost uniformly the overworked class. People in this class have learned how to economize time, and no matter how crowded their schedule, are always found capable of doing a little more. It is much easier for one who is always busy to exert himself a little more for an extra purpose than for the person who does nothing to get up steam for the same end. Give a busy man ten minutes to write a letter and he will do it at once; give an idle man a day, and he will put it off till tomorrow or next week.

The people who do the greatest things do them by steadily making moments count. Anyone who imagines that he would do great things if he only had more time is mistaken. You can find time if you will only set about doing it. Therefore, don't complain for your lack of leisure. Rather thank God that you are not cursed with leisure, for it is a curse nine times out of ten. What if you cannot find an entire month, a week, or even a day to achieve some good work that you have deeply at heart? Shall you therefore kiss it goodbye, and fold your arms in despair? Instead, endeavor to gather up the broken fragments of your time, rendered more precious by their brevity.

Set a high price on your leisure moments. Consider the sand in the hourglass as grains of precious gold. Where they work with gold the very dust of the room is carefully gathered up for the few grains of gold that may be saved. Learn from this the economy of time. Gather up life's gold dust, those bits of hours that seems so valueless singly but so immeasurable in aggregate, and you will be rich in leisure. Depend on it—if you are a miser of moments, if you utilize odd minutes, half-hours, unexpected holidays, the five minute gaps, then your careful gleanings at the end of life will have formed a large and solid block of time, and you will be wealthier in good deeds harvested than thousands whose time is all their own.

⚜

SICKNESS

Sickness takes us aside and sets us alone with God. We are taken into his private chamber, and there he talks with us face to face. The world is afar off, our relish for it is gone, and we are alone with Him. All our former props are taken away, and now we must lean on God alone. The things of earth are felt to be vanity. We are cast wholly upon God so that we may learn that his praise and his sympathy are enough.

When a person is laboring under the pain of any disease, no one is the object of his envy, admiration or contempt. But he realizes there is a need for sympathy and love between one person and another. Thus disease is an indirect blessing. One who has never known a day's illness has missed the finest lecture in that great school of humanity, the sick chamber.

It teaches humility. Our absence is scarcely noticed. From the noisy, wrestling world we are separated completely, yet our place is filled and all moves on without us. So we learn that when at last we shall sink forever beneath the waves of the sea of life, there will be but one ripple, and the current will move steadily on.

It is on the bed of sickness that we fully realize the value of good health. The first wealth is health. Health is one of the greatest blessings we are capable of enjoying. Money cannot buy it; therefore, value it, and be thankful for it. Health is above all gold and treasure.

The helplessness and weakness of the sick chamber makes a most effective appeal to the love and kindness inherent in the hearts of those who watches over and cares for the person who is afflicted.

It is on the sickbed that the heart learns most completely the value of self-examination. How strong are the resolutions for future guidance! And only God and the angels know how many lives have been turned from evil courses to the right—those who can date their progress in the good and true from some bed of sickness. We should therefore be patient in sickness. Let us utilize it to better our hearts so that we may reap from what seems unpleasant that which ultimately leads in no small degree to our happiness.

SORROW

Those who have suffered much are like those who know many languages—they have learned to understand and to be understood by all. In sorrows we love and trust our friends more tenderly.

Just as it is only at night that other worlds are to be seen shining in the distance, so it is in sorrow—the night of the soul—that we see the farthest, and know ourselves to be sons and daughters of immortality. As the rose is composed of the sweetest flowers and the sharpest thorns; as the heavens are sometime serene and sometimes overcast, so is the life of man intermingled with hopes and fears, joys and sorrows, pleasures and pains.

There are cases where the heart fails to accept the lesson taught by sorrow and suffering. A person will always be impaired by sorrow if he is not improved by it. By submission to sorrow, the sweetest traits of character are developed. Endeavor to extract a blessing from the remembrance of your own suffering. If you have not been disciplined by sorrow, strive to learn the lesson by considering the lot of those less favored than you.

We must be careful that we do not take pleasure in indulging in grief, thus converting what was a means of discipline necessary for growth into an evil that contracts life.

The winds of adversity sweep over the soul and scatter the blossoms of hope. But the blossoms fall that the fruit may appear. So it is with us, when the flowers of hope are gone, there appears the fruits of hope, patience, faith, and love. The darkest clouds that hang over human destiny appear bright to the angels who behold them from heaven.

Those who work hard seldom yield themselves entirely up to sorrow. Much of the most useful work done by men and women has been done in the middle of affliction—sometimes as a relief from it and to overpower personal sorrow. When sorrow pours upon you, instead of giving way to it, seek by occupation to divert the dark waters that threaten to overwhelm you into the many channels that the duties of life always present. Before you know it those waters will fertilize the present and give birth to flowers that will brighten the future.

POVERTY

It is not the men and women who have been reared in affluence who have left the most enduring traces on the world. It is not in the sheltered garden or greenhouse, but on the rugged Alpine cliffs where the storms beat most violently that the toughest plants are reared. It is not prosperity so much as adversity, not wealth so much as poverty that stimulates the perseverance of strong and healthy natures and develops their character.

It is the misfortune of many young people to begin life with too many advantages. Every possible want is supplied and help of every kind is lavished upon them until all ambition is extinguished. Having done nothing to earn the good things of life, they cannot appreciate their value.

Early poverty is a blessing in disguise. It is a decided advantage for a person to have to struggle with poverty and conquer it. The school of poverty graduates the ablest pupils. A triumph over poverty is like graduating with honors from West Point. It demonstrates stuff and stamina. A young person who cannot stand this test is not good for anything. Poverty saves a thousand times more people than it ruins; it saves multitudes of those whom wealth would have ruined.

It is the great privilege of poverty to be happy and unenvied, to be healthy without medicine, secure without a guard, and to obtain from the bounty of nature what the great and wealthy are compelled to procure by the help of art.

Poverty is never felt so severely as by those who have seen better days. The poverty of the poor has many elements of hardness, but it is endurable and develops their strength and endurance. The poverty of the formerly affluent is, indeed, hard. It avoids the light of the day and shuns the sympathy of those who would relieve its wants. The sunshine of life is gone, and it requires a strong mind to resolutely set about to mend the impaired fortune.

The majority of people of distinction in this country are not the sons and daughters of fathers who could give them all they wanted and much more, but are those who were brought up in cottages and cabins, cutting their way through difficulties on every side to their present commanding position.

Many of the evils of poverty are imaginary, arising from mistaken notions of what constitutes happiness and comfort. There is really not as much difference as some people imagine between the poor and the rich. In pomp, show, and opinion there is a great deal, but little as to the real pleasures and joys of life. No person is poor who does not think himself so. Home comfort and happiness does not depend upon elegance of surroundings. Thus the evils of poverty are much exaggerated. And the evils, if they are evils, are for our own ultimate good.

Poverty of the mind is the most deplorable and without excuse. Everyone can lay up a rich store of mental wealth. The poor man's purse may be empty, but he has as much gold in the sunset and as much silver in the moon as anybody. Wealth of the heart is not dependent upon wealth of the purse. Gold will not store a mind with wisdom; more likely it will fill it with folly. It may decorate the body, but it cannot adorn the soul.

FAILURE

A person builds a ship and launches it on the sea of life only to have it come back to him beaten, battered, and torn by the fury of the gale—the wreck of a first trial. The world is not coming to an end because our petty plans have miscarried. We rise highest on the ruins of our most cherished dreams, finding in our failures our real successes.

Those who risk nothing can lose nothing; sowing no hopes they cannot suffer disappointment. But let the person who is enlisted in the war expect to meet the enemy. To give way to disappointments is to invite defeat. To bravely resist them is to put them to flight, and out of temporary misfortune lay the foundation of a more glorious success.

It is a mistake to suppose that people succeed through success. More often the experience from which they gain the most lasting value is gathered from their failures. Ask a successful person and he will tell you that he learned the secret of success through being baffled, defeated, thwarted, and circumvented—far more than from his successes. Precept, study, advice, and example could never have taught him as well as failure has done. It has disciplined and taught him what to do as well as what *not* to do. And the latter is often more important than the former.

Failure in one direction has sometimes had the effect of forcing the far-seeing student to apply himself in another direction, which has in many instances proven to be just what he is fitted for. No one can tell how many of the world's most brilliant geniuses have succeeded because of their first failure.

In the military the best general is the one who from defeat organizes ultimate victory. In the battle of life the true winner is the one who even while smarting under the sting of present failure, lays his plans and summons his forces for a triumphant victory.

If you fail now and then, do not be discouraged. Remind yourself that it is the experience of every successful person. There were times when Shakespeare thought himself no poet. In fact, the most successful people have often had the most failures.

The weakling goes no farther than his first failure. By this winnowing process the number of competitors is restricted to few, and there is plenty of space in the arena for those who determine to press on. You can hardly find a successful person who won't admit that he was made so by failure and what he once thought his hard fate was in reality his good fortune. Failures are just stepping-stones, or at worst a delay of the desired end before its time.

It is the brave resolution to do better next time that lays the foundation for all true greatness. Too often, a person starts relying on the fame of past achievements while overlooking the fact that it is hard work alone that renders success certain.

We need to look at our past mistakes in the right way with a desire to learn from them. But the error people make is to attribute their failures to circumstances instead of to character. We tend to draw a veil over our imperfections and persuade ourselves that unfortunate circumstances are the entire cause of all our misfortune. It is true that circumstances aren't always favorable, yet he who is always shifting the blame for his failures upon these external causes is often the very person who has the most reason to trace them to his own inherent weaknesses.

Just as the inventor subjects his product to the most rigorous tests in order that inherent defects may become known and remedied, failure enables us to eliminate those traits of character that are a hindrance to our lasting success.

Life becomes a burden to the person who has placed his whole mind on the attainment of some object and then fails to reach it. To a young person, devastation comes like the cold dew of evening upon the flowers. However, the next morning the sun banishes the dew, and the flower is brighter and purer from its momentary affliction. But to the person of mature years, the blighting of cherished hopes falls with a chilling effect. It is hard to proceed as though nothing has happened and cheerfully take up life's load. Yet this is a test of character. To struggle and again and again renew the conflict—*this* is life's inheritance.

Above all, don't sink into apathy and despair. Rouse yourself, and don't allow your best years to slip past because you have not succeeded as you thought you would. Remember that fortune is like the skies of April, sometimes clouded and sometimes clear and favorable. It would be folly to despair of ever seeing the sun again because today is stormy. So it is equally unwise to sink into despair when fortune frowns, because she may surely be expected to smile again.

In your efforts to accomplish some great and noble work, don't be intimidated by the thought that you can never be sure of success even when steadfastly pursued at much cost. Let it be enough that the end you have in view is the right one and if you are not destined to accomplish it, then after you are gone, future generations shall enter into your labor and eat the fruit of the tree that you have planted.

What is the lesson for us to learn from this? Life is full of disappointments and it is vain to expect you will escape them. But also learn to go forward with a brave face. You may fail, but from this failure you can organize future success. Just because you were disappointed in one particular plan doesn't mean you should abandon all plans. Do not conclude, therefore, that your whole life is a failure. Rise above misfortune, and you will be rewarded by a final victory made more glorious by temporary discouragement.

SPIRITUAL LIFE

FAITH

Faith teaches man that he is a spiritual being, that he has an inward life enshrined in a material encasement—an immortal gem set for now in an earthly body. It assures man that he lives not for this life alone, but for another superior to this, more glorious and real. It teaches that God is a spirit, and seeks to worship him as such. It dignifies humanity with immortality.

There is also faith in one's own abilities. When not allowed to degenerate into egotism, it is beneficial, and necessary to enable us to make the most of life and its possibilities. Its true foundation is the same as any faith; that is, reliance on God's promise, "As you sow, so shall you reap." Hence, relying on this, and putting forth the necessary effort, why not confidently expect fulfillment of the promise?

God has given you a desire for earthly happiness. He planted in you the capacity of finding happiness in all his ways. There is not a true joy in life that you will deprive yourself of by being faithful to Him and his laws. Faith is the key that unlocks the cabinet of God's treasures.

Morality, as a guiding light to man, sometimes promotes noble ends. Surrounded by friends and the comforts of life, morality appears sufficient; but when the storms of life blow upon us, then we see how necessary it is to have faith in God's Word and his promises. Faith is necessary in the homes of the rich and the cabins of the poor.

Faith is not proved and established by logic or reason. As the flower is before the fruit, so is faith before good works. He who has faith will show it by his works.

A living, active faith is based on the belief that people should have faith in the promises of others. We need a faith in our fellowman. It is only from experience that the little child learns to distrust others. What a wilderness this would be if the confidence that exists between husband and wife were destroyed or if mutual confidence did not exist between members of the same family circle! Home would cease to be home; family ties would prove to be bonds of straw; communities could not be held together; the vast fabric of society would dissolve, and countries would once more be inhabited by barbarians.

⚜

WORSHIP

Prayer is the key to open the day, and the bolt to shut the night. Even though the sky drops the morning and evening dew upon the grass, it would not grow green unless a great shower at certain seasons supplied the rest. So devotion to prayer twice a day is like the falling of the early and the evening dew. But if you would flourish in works of grace, empty the great clouds sometimes and let fall a full shower of prayer.

Even from the deepest dungeon, a good man's prayer will climb heaven's height and bring a

180

blessing down. Between the humble and contrite heart and the Majesty of heaven there are no barriers. The only password is prayer. Prayer is a shield to the sword, a sacrifice to God, and a scourge to Satan.

Prayer is not eloquence, but earnestness; not the definition of helplessness, but the feeling of it—the language of the soul. When the heart is full and bitter thoughts come crowding thickly up for utterance, how much the bursting heart may relieve itself in prayer!

The custom of having family prayers is the one thing which more than any other knits together the loose threads of a home, and unites its members before God. Family worship in which parents, children, and friends daily join in praise and prayer is an acknowledgment of dependence on the Heavenly Father and a renewal of dedication to his work in the world. The Bible is read, a hymn is sung, a petition is offered. The sick and the absent are remembered; the tempted and the tried are commended to God. Unless all has been done as a mere formality and without hearty assent, those who have gathered at the family altar leave it helped, soothed, strengthened, and armored as they were not before they met there. As the Israelites in the desert were attended by the pillar and cloud, so in life's wilderness the family who inquires of the Lord is constantly overshadowed by his presence and love.

There may be times when we ask in prayer for something that would harm us and the Father denies us for our own good. Or we may even pray for trivial things, without even thinking of the greatest blessings. Good prayers never come creeping home. We will receive either what we ask for or what we should ask for. No person ever prayed heartily without learning something.

It is for our sake, not God's sake, that worship and prayer are required. Not that God may be rendered more gracious, but that man may be made better and reminded of his dependent state.

God does not respect the arithmetic of our prayers, how many they are; nor the rhetoric of our prayers, how neat they are; nor the geometry of our prayers, how long they are; nor the music of our prayers, how melodious they are; nor the logic of our prayers, how methodical they are; but whether they truly originate from the heart. We should pray with as much earnestness as those who expect everything from God, and act with as much energy as those who expect everything from themselves. When we pray for any virtue we should cultivate the virtue as well as pray for it.

It is not everyone who is able to pray in the hearing of others with ease. The timid tongue falters, and the thought struggles in vain for utterance. But who cannot read a psalm or a chapter or a few verses, and while kneeling repeat with tender trust the Lord's Prayer? When we think of it, that includes everything.

THE BIBLE

The Bible is a book whose words live in the ear like music that can never be forgotten. It should be part of the national mind.

It reveals to us the character and wisdom of our great Creator and Final Judge. It opens before us the way of salvation through a Redeemer, unveils to our view the invisible world, and shows us the final destiny of our soul. God's Word is, in fact, much like God's world, varied, very rich, and very beautiful. You'll never exhaust all its merits.

The Bible has something for every class of people. The Bible goes equally to the cottage of the poor man and the palace of the king. It has taken hold of the world as no other book ever did.

It is the foundation of our religious faith and our practical daily guide as well. It blends itself with our daily conversation, and is the silver thread of all our best reading, giving its hue to books, magazines, newspapers, and the media. On the seas it goes with the mariner as his spiritual chart and compass, and on the land it is to untold millions their pillar of cloud by day and their column of fire by night.

In the home and in the world, amid temptation and trials, the Bible is man's most faithful attendant and his strongest shield. Stand before it as before a mirror, and you will see there not only your good traits, but also your errors, follies, and sins, which you did not imagine until you thus examined yourself. If you desire to make constant improvement, go to the Bible.

There is no book so well adapted to improve both the head and the heart as the Bible. It is a *tried* book. Its utility is demonstrated by experience; its necessity is confessed by all who have studied the wants of human nature. It has wrung reluctant praise even from the lips of its foes. Other books tell of their own age; the Bible was made for all ages. The Bible reveals truths before unknown, and otherwise unknowable. It is distinguished for its exact and universal truth. Time and criticism only illustrate and confirm its pages. Successive ages reveal nothing to change the Bible's representation of human nature. Passing events fulfill its prophecies, but fail to impeach its allegations.

The cheerless gloom that broods over the understandings of man has never been chased away but for the beams of supernatural revelation. People may look with an unfriendly eye on that system of truth that reproves and condemns them; but they little know the loss the world would sustain by subverting its foundations. We have tried paganism, Mohammedanism, Deism and philosophy, and we cannot look upon any of them with respect. The Scriptures contain the only system of truth that is available to us, and if we give it up, we have no other worthy to replace it.

The Scriptures teach us the best way of living, the noblest way of suffering, and the most comfortable way of dying.

GOD IN NATURE

God writes the Gospel not in the Bible alone, but on trees and flowers and clouds and stars. All nature speaks a language that makes it easy to understand the majesty and power of its Author. Those things which nature is said to do are done by divine art, using nature as an instrument. Nature is the chart of God, marking out all his attributes. A beautiful harmony runs through all of God's works.

Nature is like a book that is ever open before us displaying a variety of lessons for our instruction every day. It invites us to read and all that it requires of us is the will to do so; with eyes to see, with ears to hear, with hearts and souls to feel, and with minds to comprehend. Infinite intelligence was required to compose this mighty volume, which never fails to impart the highest wisdom to those who study it with willing hearts and humble minds. He who attentively studies nature and fails to see in her ways the workings of Providence must, indeed, be blind.

FUTURE LIFE

Are we to live after death and if we are, in what state? These are questions confined to no climate, creed, or community. It matters little what their present surroundings are. If poverty and pain are their lot, they know that rest will come to them later. Those who do not possess this pleasing hope of immortality feel at times a painful longing, a vague unrest. To them, the future is dark and uncertain, and there are times when they would willingly give all they have just to see a beacon of light or feel the strong assurance of faith that they would live again. If only they would see clearly under the guiding light of Christianity, the future would be full of hope for them.

Surely there is reasonable ground for this hope! Among the most effectual and most beautiful reasons for the hope that there is a life beyond the grave is derived from the change of the seasons. The new life that bursts forth in Spring in objects apparently dead calls upon our faith to believe that this also will be our destiny. The trees that have faded and remained dark and gray through the long, dreary winter clothe themselves again with green in the spring, and everything we see rekindles to life. It cannot be that earth is man's only abiding place. We are bound for a higher destiny than that of earth.

As death approaches and this world recedes, we clearly see that spiritual world in which we have been living all along, though we knew it not. The dying man tells us of attendant angels hovering around him. They might have been with him all through life, but he didn't see them. There is a glorious light that rests on the countenance of one whose soul has just departed to heaven.

THE EVENING OF LIFE

The hourglass is truly an emblem of the world around us. As its sands run out, so it shows that all things must have an end. It is only on the border of eternity that the fleeting period of our life on earth is comprehended.

We must at some time or other enter the last year of our life when we will fight the battle with the last enemy. There are many memorable years in history, as in them died men and women of renown; but the year of our death will be more memorable to us than any. That year will open with the usual New-year's congratulations; it will rejoice in the same orchard blossoming, and the sweet fragrances of Spring. It will witness the golden glory of the harvest, and the merry-makings of Christmas. And yet to us it will be vastly different because it will be our closing year. It will be the year in which our body and soul part— the year in which for us, time ends and eternity begins.

In the light of eternity, how vain and foolish appear the contentions and troubles of mankind! Addison most beautifully expresses this thought in these lines; "When I look upon the tombs of the great, every emotion of envy dies; when I read the epitaph of the beautiful, every inordinate desire forsakes me; when I meet with the grief of parents upon a tombstone, my heart melts with compassion; when I see the tombs of the parents themselves, I reflect how vain it is to grieve for those we must quickly follow; when I see kings lying beside those who deposed them, when I see rivals placed side by side, or the holy men who divided the world with their contests and disputes, I reflect with sorrow and astonishment on the frivolous competitions, factions, and debates of mankind."

There is a beauty in age. The morning of life may be glowing with the expectations of youth; the noon may be fruitful in endeavors and works; but the evening of life is the time of rest and reflection. When young, it is natural to lay out ambitious plans. How easy it seems to achieve any wished-for thing! But after being confronted by the stern realities of life, it's easy to lose sight of the dreams of youth.

If our time is used wisely, we won't regret that childhood's days are passed. We are men and women engaged in doing what God has assigned to us. This is the time of life that we would most willingly see prolonged. But time doesn't stop in it and in vain we protest. The sun as swiftly descends to its setting as it rose to its noon. The elasticity of youth gives way to the carefully measured steps of age, and on the head, time sprinkles its snow. The form that so rapidly matured into one of grace, strength and character is bowed by the weight of years.

Old age, like solitude and sorrow, has its revelations, and we can muse over the events of past years and perceive the hollowness of many of the bubbles we have been pursuing. We can also contemplate the mysteries of the future. The most momentous period of life is about at hand—that time when we will exchange this life for another. What age can there be more important than this? It is natural for youth to regard old age as a dreary season—one that admits very little that can be called pleasure. They don't understand that age offers different kinds of enjoyments and it is no less pleasant than any other season of life.

Age shouldn't cause anxiety to those who see it near because experience proves that it abounds with consolations and its own delights. The world in general bows down to age, gives it preference, and listens with respect to its opinions. Such reverence must be soothing to age, and compensates it for the loss of many of the enjoyments of youth.

How many would wish to live again in the past? If we could return and carry with us our present experience, all would wish to do so. The number of those whose life has been so happy that they would wish to live it over again is exceedingly small. Your present experience will remain with you through life. And hence, even though old age appears to us now to be devoid of pleasure, we will find that when the passage of years brings us to that point we will not willingly exchange it for any of the stages of life gone by.

In the light of eternity, does it make any great difference whether our existence has passed surrounded with the comforts of wealth or struggling for the necessities of life? We are all equal in death; the king and the peasant, the rich and the poor are all alike in this respect—it is the common lot of humanity.

Age is the beautiful closing scene of earthly life, death the entrance to life immortal. We ought to live wisely so that it is the final triumph of a well-lived life.

APPENDIX

As I was finishing this book, the following story was forwarded to me by a friend, Steve Nielson, in an e-mail. It illustrates many of the principles covered in this book. See if you can pick them out as you read.

THE DAFFODIL PRINCIPLE***

Several times my daughter had telephoned to say, "Mother, you must come to see the daffodils before they are over." I wanted to go, but it was a two-hour drive from Laguna to Lake Arrowhead. "I will come next Tuesday," I promised a little reluctantly on her third call.

Next Tuesday dawned cold and rainy. Still, I had promised, and reluctantly I drove there. When I finally walked into Carolyn's house I was welcomed by the joyful sounds of happy children. I delightedly hugged and greeted my grandchildren.

"Forget the daffodils, Carolyn! The road is invisible in these clouds and fog, and there is nothing in the world except you and these children that I want to see badly enough to drive another inch!"

My daughter smiled calmly and said, "We drive in this all the time, Mother."

"Well, you won't get me back on the road until it clears, and then I'm heading for home!" I assured her.

"But first we're going to see the daffodils. It's just a few blocks," Carolyn said. "I'll drive. I'm used to this."

"Carolyn," I said sternly, "please turn around."

"It's all right, Mother, I promise. You will never forgive yourself if you miss this experience."

After about twenty minutes, we turned onto a small gravel road and I saw a small church. On the far side of the church, I saw a hand lettered sign with an arrow that read, "Daffodil Garden." We got out of the car, each took a child's hand, and I followed Carolyn down the path. Then, as we turned a corner, I looked up and gasped. Before me lay the most glorious sight.

It looked as though someone had taken a great vat of gold and poured it over the mountain peak and its surrounding slopes. The flowers were planted in majestic, swirling patterns, great ribbons and swaths of deep orange, creamy white, lemon yellow, salmon pink, and saffron and butter yellow. Each different-colored variety was planted in large groups so that it swirled and flowed like its own river with its own unique hue. There were five acres of flowers.

"Who did this?" I asked Carolyn.

"Just one woman," Carolyn answered. "She lives on the property. That's her home." Carolyn pointed to a well-kept A-frame house, small and modestly sitting in the midst of all that glory. We walked up to the house.

On the patio, we saw a poster. "Answers to the Questions I Know You Are Asking" was the headline. The first answer was a simple one. "50,000 bulbs," it read. The second answer was, "One at a time, by one woman. Two hands, two feet, and one brain." The third answer was, "Began in 1958."

For me, that moment was a life-changing experience. I thought of this woman whom I had never met, who, more than forty years before, had begun, one bulb at a time, to bring her vision of beauty and joy to an obscure mountaintop. Planting one bulb at a time, year after year, this unknown woman had forever changed the world in which she lived. One day at a time, she had created something of extraordinary magnificence, beauty, and inspiration. The principle her daffodil garden taught is one of the greatest principles of celebration.

That is, learning to move toward our goals and desires one step at a time—often just one baby-step at time—and learning to love the doing, learning to use the accumulation of time. When we multiply tiny pieces of time with small increments of daily effort, we too will find we can accomplish magnificent things. We can change the world.

"It makes me sad in a way," I admitted to Carolyn. "What might I have accomplished if I had thought of a wonderful goal thirty-five or forty years ago and had worked away at it 'one bulb at a time' through all those years? Just think what I might have been able to achieve!"

My daughter summed up the message of the day in her usual direct way. "Start tomorrow," she said.

She was right. It's so pointless to think of the lost hours of yesterdays. The way to make this a lesson of celebration instead of a cause for regret is to only ask, "How can I put this to use today?"

Use the Daffodil Principle. Stop waiting...

Until your car or home is paid off
Until you get a new car or home
Until your kids leave the house
Until you go back to school
Until you finish school
Until you clean the house
Until you organize the garage
Until you clean off your desk
Until you lose 10 lbs
Until you gain 10 lbs.
Until you get married
Until you get a divorce
Until you have kids
Until the kids go to school
Until you retire
Until summer
Until spring
Until winter
Until fall
Until you die...

There is no better time than right now to be happy.

Happiness is a journey, not a destination. So work like you don't need money. Love like you've never been hurt. Dance like no one's watching.

Don't be afraid that your life will end, be afraid that it will never begin.

⚜

I believe that the wellspring of all virtues is honesty, not only in the big things, but the little things as well. I hope this story drives this point home to you and me.

THE SEED

A successful Christian businessman was growing old and knew it was time to choose a successor to take over the business. Instead of choosing one of his directors or his children, he decided to do something different. He called all the young executives in his company together.

He said, "It is time for me to step down and choose the next CEO. I have decided to choose one of you. "The young executives were shocked, but the boss continued. "I am going to give each one of you a SEED today - one very special SEED. I want you to plant the seed, water it, and come back here one year from today with what you have grown from the seed I have given you. I will then judge the plants that you bring, and the one I choose will be the next CEO."

One man, named Jim, was there that day and he, like the others, received a seed. He went home and excitedly, told his wife the story. She helped him get a pot, soil and compost and he planted the seed. Everyday, he would water it and watch to see if it had grown. After about three weeks, some of the other executives began to talk about their seeds and the plants that were beginning to grow. Jim kept checking his seed, but nothing ever grew. Three weeks, four weeks, five weeks went by, still nothing. By now, others were talking about their plants, but Jim didn't have a plant and he felt like a failure.

Six months went by—still nothing in Jim's pot. He just knew he had killed his seed. Everyone else had trees and tall plants, but he had nothing. Jim didn't say anything to his colleagues, however. He just kept watering and fertilizing the soil - He so wanted the seed to grow.

A year finally went by and all the young executives of the company brought their plants to the CEO for inspection. Jim told his wife that he wasn't going to take an empty pot. But she asked him to be honest about what happened. Jim felt sick at his stomach, it was going to be the most embarrassing moment of his life, but he knew his wife was right. He took his empty pot to the boardroom. When Jim arrived, he was amazed at the variety of plants grown by the other executives. They were beautiful—in all shapes and sizes. Jim put his empty pot on the floor and many of his colleagues laughed, a few felt sorry for him!

When the CEO arrived, he surveyed the room and greeted his young executives. Jim just tried to hide in the back. "My, what great plants, trees, and flowers you have grown," said the CEO. "Today one of you will be appointed the next CEO!" All of a sudden, the CEO spotted Jim at the back of the room with his empty pot. He ordered the financial director to bring him to the front. Jim was terrified. He thought, "The CEO knows I'm a failure! Maybe he will have me fired!"

When Jim got to the front, the CEO asked him what had happened to his seed - Jim told him the story. The CEO asked everyone to sit down except Jim. He looked at Jim, and then announced to the young executives, "Behold your next Chief Executive! His name is Jim!" Jim couldn't believe it. Jim couldn't even grow his seed. How could he be the new CEO the others said?

Then the CEO said, "One year ago today, I gave everyone in this room a seed. I told you to take the seed, plant it, water it, and bring it back to me today. But I gave you all boiled seeds; they were dead – it was not possible for them to grow. All of you, except Jim, have brought me trees and plants and flowers. When you found that the seed would not grow, you substituted another seed for the one I gave you. Jim was the only one with the courage and honesty to bring me a pot with my seed in it. Therefore, he is the one who will be the new Chief Executive!"

Remember...

If you plant honesty, you will reap trust

If you plant goodness, you will reap friends

If you plant humility, you will reap greatness

If you plant perseverance, you will reap contentment

If you plant consideration, you will reap perspective

If you plant hard work, you will reap success

If you plant forgiveness, you will reap reconciliation

If you plant faith in Christ, you will reap a harvest

So, be careful what you plant now; it will determine what you reap later.

www.ingramcontent.com/pod-product-compliance
Lightning Source LLC
Chambersburg PA
CBHW031317040426
42443CB00005B/110